LEED v4
GREEN ASSOCIATE MOCK EXAMS
Questions, Answers, and Explanations

A Must-Have for LEED Exams, Green Building LEED
Certification, and Sustainability
Green Associate Exam Guide Series

GANG CHEN

ArchiteG®, Inc.
Irvine, California

LEED v4 GREEN ASSOCIATE MOCK EXAMS:
Questions, Answers, and Explanations: A Must-Have for LEED Exams, Green Building LEED Certification, and Sustainability. Green Associate Exam Guide Series

Copyright © 2021　　Gang Chen
V1
Cover Photo © 2021　Gang Chen

Copy Editor: Penny L Kortje

All Rights Reserved.
No part of this book may be transmitted or reproduced by any means or in any form, including electronic, graphic, or mechanical, without the express written consent of the publisher or author, except in the case of brief quotations in a review.

ArchiteG®, Inc.
http://www.ArchiteG.com

ISBN: 978-1-61265-046-3

PRINTED IN THE UNITED STATES OF AMERICA

What others are saying about "LEED GREEN ASSOCIATE Mock Exam"…

"GREAT STUDY TOOL!!!
"My friend had told me about this book a week before my 2nd exam (yes I failed it the first time by one point could you believe it?) and it was a great learning tool! It really asked thorough questions and gave detailed explanations to the answers. If you can do good on these mock exams, you will do great on the real test! This guide really makes you utilize your knowledge and skill, other materials I had purchased prior to this were quite vague and uninformative, but this did the trick! Thanks Gang!"
—Jason

"Good book...
"I just pass the test with 183. The questions are more difficult that the ones that I saw in the test...That is good if you want to be sure that you will pass..."
—Omar Reyes

"Nailed that LEED GREEN ASSOCIATE on the first try!
"With this book, plus the 'LEED Green Associate Exam Guide' (also by Gang Chen) combined with all the free .PDF downloads printed from the USGBC website, I passed my LEED GREEN ASSOCIATE exam on the first attempt! This little book has 2 full mock-exams you can test yourself on throughout your studying to gauge when you are primed & ready to take the exam...Highly recommended."
—Sarah Bartz

"Excellent Guide, Tougher than the Actual Exam!
"I found this and the supplemental 'LEED Green Associate Exam Guide' to be extraordinarily helpful. I read both books and glanced at a couple online documents, but otherwise I relied purely on this book and passed with flying colors. I scored about a 65% on both mock exams the day before I took the exam and scored about a 91% on the actual thing. I was more than prepared for the LEED Green Associate Exam and couldn't be happier. I'll take a pass any day! Also, I think that these exams, while not flawless, help you on your way to become a LEED AP with Specialty, helping make sure you know MORE than is needed on this first, easier part of the exam. I would definitely recommend this and the accompanying guide, especially if you're on a tight schedule (I budgeted two weeks over the Thanksgiving holiday and found it to be a pretty good time table). Good luck and think Green!"
—Austin Curtiss Rice

"Such a great tool
"I passed the exam at the first attempt. These mock exams helped me to learn how to tackle the problems and which areas I should focus on! I worked with another book of the author also. It took 2-3 weeks for my preparation."
—Chai

"Great news, I passed!!!
"'LEED GREEN ASSOCIATE Mock Exams' is a great book for assessing progress in your efforts to

study and pass the LEED Green Associate Exam. Not only is it a method of testing and self assessment, but it is also an educational tool. Personally, I found that using 'LEED GREEN ASSOCIATE Mock Exams' helped in my passing the LEED Green Associate Exam on the first attempt because it tested me on the portions of the exam that seemed more obscure and slightly harder than others. The book doubles as an educational medium because of the answer explanations. There isn't simply a list of correct answers in the back of the book. However, there are deep rooted explanations accompanying the correct answer choice. As an educator and business professional I would absolutely recommend this book to anyone looking to take and pass the LEED GREEN ASSOCIATE exam on the first attempt. I found using this book in conjunction with other study materials was what afforded me the ability of passing the LEED GREEN ASSOCIATE exam. Good luck in passing your LEED GREEN ASSOCIATE exam and buy this book!"
—Luke Ferland

"Preparing for LEED GREEN ASSOCIATE Exam
"This book provides several key points that I think will be crucial in my preparation for taking the LEED Green Associate Exam in the next month. Like many similar test prep guides, Mr. Chen cites the resources that will be useful to study. But he goes beyond this and differentiates which ones must memorize and those you must be at least familiar with. In this way, he is trying to give you the tools to streamline your

study efforts for the best results. He is very aware that most individuals looking to take this exam are already working a 40-hour week and he wants you to invest your time wisely and efficiently.

Throughout this book Mr. Chen stresses that the primary keys to success are 1) to study in such a way that builds your confidence and 2) to time the taking of the exam so that this knowledge is still present in your consciousness. I am looking forward to also reading his 'LEED Green Associate Exam Guide.'"
—**NPacella**

"Review of Gang Chen's LEED GREEN ASSOCIATE Mock Exams
"Studying for any LEED exam is an arduous task. Chen's 'LEED GREEN ASSOCIATE Mock Exams' is a good study aid in helping you prepare for the LEED GREEN ASSOCIATE exam. The questions are designed to test your understanding of the principles; and the answers found at the end of the section provide further explanation so you can better grasp the principle. This is a great way to reinforce your memory. Read 'LEED GREEN ASSOCIATE Mock Exams' before you start studying other resource materials. It will serve to bring your attention to the information that you are most likely to be asked on the exam as you come across it in your studying.

I also found the information and links to other resources very helpful. It is a comprehensive list of "must read" information for anyone studying for the

LEED exams. Chen has done the research and review to provide the ones that will be most useful.

I found his 'LEED GREEN ASSOCIATE Mock Exams' easy to read and use and recommend it to anyone preparing for the LEED GREEN ASSOCIATE exam."
—Mike Kwon

"Helpful Practice Exams
"I am in the process of studying for the LEED GREEN ASSOCIATE exam and have been finding overall that there is a confusing array of study guides and suggestions from USGBC. This brought me to look for other study outlets and I was glad to find this book. It is very clear and easy to use. The book is written in a succinct and easy to digest form and has clarified some confusing points. The book contains two full practice exams. The answer key has detailed explanations for each correct point. The book also includes frequently asked questions, and appendixes with useful additional resources. There is also an index which makes it very easy to look up issues. I would recommend this book to someone who is looking for practice exams for the LEED GREEN ASSOCIATE test."
—Green Danny

"LEED as a language
"LEED is a language, a new way of 'speaking' (and thinking) about our relationship to our world in general and our buildings in particular. This new language, as with all things new, presents challenges to

the established order - in my case the order of my professional practice.

Gang Chen's new book, 'LEED GREEN ASSOCIATE Mock Exams' is proving itself to be an excellent training tool for me as I learn to master the language of LEED.

A recent NY Times article (Personal Best - the Secrets of Elite Athletes - 18 Oct 2010 made the following observations,

"Elite runners will examine a course, running it before they race it..."

'LEED GREEN ASSOCIATE Mock Exams' is designed to concentrate on increasing the intensity of your study efforts, examine the course, run it before you race it - providing the format and substance for the practice that leads to the experience needed to get this new language right."

—Howard Patrick (Pat) Barry, AIA NCARB, Barry Associates Architects

"On the tougher side

"I found these exams to be quite tougher compared to the others I took a look at, which is good as it made me prepare for the worst I would definitely recommend using these mock exams. Also, in-depth explanations at the end make your basics quite clear. I ultimately passed with 181 with 3 weeks of study. Best wishes to all."

—swankysenor

"Great Resource!!!!!!
"This book is a great resource for anyone studying for the LEED GREEN ASSOCIATE exam!!! Almost as important as learning the material is learning to 'test well.' Learning to read a test question and think clearly in the testing environment is critically important for passing the LEED GREEN ASSOCIATE exam as well as the LEED AP with specialty exams."
—Charles

Leadership in Energy and Environmental Design (LEED)

LEED-CERTIFIED   LEED-SILVER
LEED-GOLD   LEED-PLATINUM

LEED GREEN ASSOCIATE

LEED AP BD+C   LEED AP ID+C
LEED AP O+M
LEED AP HOMES   LEED AP ND

LEED FELLOW

Dedication

To my parents, Zhuixian and Yugen,
my wife Xiaojie, and my daughters
Alice, Angela, Amy, and Athena.

Disclaimer

LEED GREEN ASSOCIATE Mock Exams provides general information about the LEED Green Associate Exam and LEED green building certification. The book is sold with the understanding that neither the publisher nor the author is providing legal, accounting, or other professional services. If legal, accounting, or other professional services are required, seek the assistance of a competent professional firm.

The purpose of this publication is not to reprint the content of all other available texts on the subject. You are urged to read other materials, and tailor them to fit your needs.

Great effort has been taken to make this resource as complete and accurate as possible; however, nobody is perfect, and there may be several typographical errors or other mistakes. You should use this book as a general guide and not as the ultimate source on this subject. If you find any potential errors, please send an e-mail to:
info@ArchiteG.com

LEED GREEN ASSOCIATE Mock Exams is intended to provide general, entertaining, informative, educational, and enlightening content. Neither the publisher nor the author shall be liable to anyone or any entity for any loss or damages, or alleged loss and damages, caused directly or indirectly by the content of this book.

USGBC and LEED are trademarks of the U.S. Green Building Council. The U.S. Green Building Council is not affiliated with this publication.

Contents

Preface

Chapter One: LEED GREEN ASSOCIATE Mock Exam A: Questions, Answers, and Explanations 25

 I. LEED GREEN ASSOCIATE Mock Exam A
 II. Answers and Explanations for the LEED GREEN ASSOCIATE Mock Exam A

Chapter Two: LEED GREEN ASSOCIATE Mock Exam B: Questions, Answers, and Explanations 81

 I. Important Note: Read this before you work on LEED GREEN ASSOCIATE Mock Exam B
   1. How much time should you spend on preparing for the LEED exam?
 II. LEED GREEN ASSOCIATE Mock Exam B
 III. Answers and Explanations for the LEED GREEN ASSOCIATE Mock Exam B
 IV. How were the LEED Green Associate Mock Exams created?

V. Where can I find the latest official sample questions for the LEED Green Associate Exam?
VI. LEED Green Associate Exam registration
  1. How do I register for the LEED Green Associate Exam?
  2. Important Note

Chapter Three: Frequently Asked Questions (FAQ) and Other Useful Resources   141

1. I found the reference guide way too tedious. Can I read your books only and just refer to the USGBC reference guide (if one is available for the exam I am taking) when needed?
2. Is one week really enough time for me to prepare for the exam while I am working?
3. Would you say that if I buy books from your LEED Exam Guide series, I could pass the exam without any other study materials? The books sold on the USGBC website cost hundreds of dollars, so I would be quite happy if I could buy your books and just use them.
4. I am preparing for the LEED exam. Do I need to read the 2" thick reference guide?
5. For LEED v4, will the total number of points be more than 110 if a project receives all of the extra and standard credits?

6. For the exam, do I need to know the project phase in which a specific prerequisite/credit takes place? i.e., pre-design, schematic design, etc.
7. Are you writing any other books for the new LEED exams? What new books are you writing?
8. Important Documents that You Need to Download for <u>Free</u>, Become Familiar with, and <u>Memorize</u>
9. Important Documents that You Need to Download for <u>Free</u>, and Become <u>Familiar</u> with

Appendixes 151
1. Default Occupancy Factors
2. Important Resources and Further Study Materials You Can Download for <u>Free</u> or at a Low Price
3. Annotated Bibliography
4. Valuable Websites and Links

Back Page Promotion 157
1. *Architectural Practice Simplified*
2. *Planting Design Illustrated*
3. LEED Exam Guide series (**GreenExamEducation**.com)

Index 177

Preface

LEED GREEN ASSOCIATE Mock Exams is a companion to *LEED Green Associate Exam Guide*. There are two main purposes for *LEED GREEN ASSOCIATE Mock Exams*: to help you pass the LEED Green Associate Exam and to assist you in understanding the process of getting a building LEED certified.

The USGBC released LEED v4 in GreenBuild International Conference and Expo in November, 2013. The GBCI started to include the new LEED v4 content for all LEED exams in June 2014. We have incorporated the new LEED v4 content in this book.

The LEED Green Associate Exam is the most important LEED exam for two reasons:

1. You have to pass this exam in order to get the title of LEED Green Associate.

2. This exam is also the required <u>Part One</u> (2 hours) of <u>ALL</u> LEED AP+ exams. You have to pass the LEED Green Associate Exam plus Part Two (2 hours) of the specific LEED AP+ exam of your choice to get any LEED AP+ title, unless you have passed the old LEED

AP Exam before June 30, 2009.

There are a few ways to prepare for the LEED Green Associate Exam:

1. You can take USGBC courses or workshops in person. You should take USGBC classes at both the 100 (Awareness) and 200 (LEED Core Concepts and Strategies) levels to successfully prepare for the exam. A one-day course can cost $450 if you register early enough, the course can be as expensive as $500 if you miss the early bird special. You also have to wait until the USGBC workshops or courses are offered in a city near you.

OR

2. Take USGBC online courses. You can go to the USGBC or GBCI websites for information. The USGBC online courses are less personal but still expensive.

OR

3. Read related books. Unfortunately, there are NO official GBCI books on the LEED Green Associate Exam. However, there are a few third-party books on the exam. *LEED Green Associate Exam Guide* and *LEED GREEN ASSOCIATE Mock Exams* are two of the first books to cover this subject and will assist you with passing the exam.

To stay at the forefront of LEED and the green building movement and to make my books more valuable to their readers, I sign up and complete USGBC courses and workshops. I also review the USGBC and GBCI websites, and many other sources to acquire as much information as possible on LEED. *LEED Green Associate Exam Guide* and *LEED GREEN ASSOCIATE Mock Exams* are a result of this very comprehensive research. I have done the hard work, so that you can save time preparing for the exam by reading my books.

Strategy 101 for the LEED Green Associate Exam is that you must recognize that you have only a limited amount of time to prepare for the exam. So, you must concentrate your time and effort on the most important content of the LEED Green Associate Exam. To assist you in achieving this goal, *LEED Green Associate Exam Guide* is broken down into two major sections: (1) the study materials and (2) the sample questions.

LEED GREEN ASSOCIATE Mock Exams provides you with two additional mock exams, including questions, answers, and explanations.

Most people already have some knowledge of LEED. I suggest that when you read this book for the first time, you should use a highlighter to mark the content that you are unfamiliar with. This way, when you do your review later and read the book for the second time, you can focus on the portions that you are unfamiliar with and save yourself a lot of time. You can repeat this process with different colored highlighters on subsequent reads until you are very familiar with the content of this book. Preparing in this manner will get you ready to take the LEED Green Associate Exam.

The key to passing the LEED Green Associate Exam, or any other exam, is to understand the scope of the exam, and not read too many books. Select one or two really good books and focus on them. Actually <u>understand</u> and <u>memorize</u> the content.

There is a part of the LEED Green Associate Exam that you can score highly on by reading study materials. You should try to answer all questions related to this part correctly.

There is also a part of the exam that you may not be able to prepare for. If you have not done actual LEED building certification, there will be some questions that may require you to guess. This could potentially be the hardest part of the exam, but these questions should be only a small percentage of the overall test and there should be no concern if you are well prepared. You should <u>eliminate</u> the obvious wrong answers and then attempt to make an educated <u>guess</u>. There is no penalty for guessing. If you have no idea what the correct answer is and cannot eliminate any obvious wrong answers, then just pick a guess answer and do not waste too much time on the question. The key is to try and use the <u>same</u> guess answer for all of the questions that you have no idea about. For example, if you choose "d" as your guess answer, then you should be consistent and use "d" as your guess answer for all the questions that you have no idea about. This way, you will likely have a better chance at guessing more correct answers.

The actual LEED Green Associate Exam has 100 multiple-choice questions and you must finish within 2 hours. The raw exam score is converted to a scaled score ranging from 125 to 200. The passing score is 170 or higher. You need to answer <u>about</u> 60 questions correctly to pass. There is an optional 10-minute tutorial for computer testing before the exam and an optional 10-minute exit survey.

This is not an easy exam, but you should be able to pass if you prepare well. If you <u>set your goal for a high score and study hard</u>, you will have a better chance of passing. If you set your goal for the minimum passing score of 170, you will probably end up scoring 169, fail, and have to <u>retake</u> the exam again. Failing will be the last thing you want. Give yourself plenty of time and do not wait until the last minute to begin preparing for the exam. I have met people who have spent 10 hours preparing and passed the exam, but I suggest that you give yourself <u>at least two to three weeks</u> of preparation time. On the night before the exam, you should look through the mock exam questions you answered incorrectly and review the correct solutions. Read this book carefully, prepare well, relax, and put yourself in the best physical, mental, and psychological state on the day of the exam. Follow this advice and you will pass the exam.

See all our books at **GreenExamEducation**.com

Check out FREE tips on the easiest way to pass the LEED Green Associate Exam and info for all LEED Exams and ARE Exams at **GeeForum.com**, you can post your questions for other users' review.

Chapter 1
LEED GREEN ASSOCIATE Mock Exam A:
Questions, Answers, and Explanations

Use the questions from the mock exams to prepare for the real exam. They will give you an idea of what the GBCI is looking for on the LEED Green Associate Exam, and how the questions will be asked. These questions are quite easy. If you can answer 60% of the sample questions correctly, you are ready to take the real exam. The 60% passing score is based on feedback from previous readers. You should read the study material in *LEED Green Associate Exam Guide* at least three times before you attempt the mock exams. Similar to the real exam, a question might ask you to pick one, two, or three correct answers out of four, or four correct answers out of five (some LEED exam questions have five choices). Generally speaking, if you do not know any of the correct answers, then you will probably get the overall answer wrong. You need to know the LEED system very well in order to answer correctly.

I have intentionally included some questions that you may not know the answers to. This is to help you practice making an educated guess.

I. LEED GREEN ASSOCIATE Mock Exam A

1. With regard to the credit, Optimize Energy Performance, who has the most influence in decision-making?
   a. MEP Engineer
   b. Architect
   c. Contractor
   d. Health Department Plan Checker

2. A project team should include the following as part of process energy: (Choose 3)
   a. Lighting that is part of the medical equipment
   b. Lighting included as part of the lighting power allowance
   c. Energy for water pumps
   d. HVAC
   e. Energy for elevators and escalators

3. A project team should include the following as part of regulated (non-process) energy: (Choose 3)
   a. Lighting for interiors
   b. Refrigeration and kitchen cooking
   c. Space heating
   d. Service water heating
   e. Energy for computers, office, and general miscellaneous equipment

4. With regard to LEED v4, which of the following LEED rating systems has fewer

points for the WE category? (Choose 2)
a. LEED BDC NC
b. LEED BDC CS
c. LEED BDC Schools
d. LEED IDC CI
e. LEED OM EB

5. Which of the following are not considered laws?
a. USGBC LEED reference guides
b. Building codes
c. ADA
d. Municipal codes
e. EPA Codes of Federal Regulations

6. Which of the following buildings cannot obtain LEED certification? (Choose 2)
a. A new building that uses CFC
b. A new building that does not use CFC
c. A remodel project with a plan to phase out CFCs in 15 years
d. A building that uses natural refrigerants
e. A building that uses dry ice

7. Which of the following can reduce stormwater runoff and alleviate the urban heat island effect? (Choose 3)
a. Increasing the site coverage ratio
b. Increasing Floor Area Ratio (FAR)
c. Using a vegetated roof
d. Using porous pavement with high albedo
e. Building a retention pond on the site

8. Recycled materials will contribute to which of the following?
   a. Traffic alleviation and smog reduction
   b. Protection of virgin materials
   c. Energy savings
   d. MEP cost savings

9. Which of the following is not graywater?
   a. Water from kitchen sinks
   b. Water from toilet
   c. Harvest rainwater
   d. Water from outdoor area drains
   e. None of above
   f. All of above

10. Which of the following is not blackwater? (Choose 2)
    a. Water from kitchen sinks
    b. Water from toilets
    c. Harvest rainwater
    d. Water from floor drains
    e. Rainwater that has come into contact with animal waste

11. Which of the following is not true? (Choose 2)
    a. Water from kitchen sinks can be reused for landscape irrigation or flushing toilets.
    b. Water from kitchen sinks cannot be reused for landscape irrigation or flushing toilets.

c. Reclaimed water requires special piping with a different color.
   d. Reclaimed water cannot reduce potable water use.

12. Which of the following sets the baseline for water use? (Choose 2)
    a. Energy Policy Act (EPAct) of 1992
    b. Uniform Plumbing Code (UPC)
    c. WaterSense standards
    d. International Plumbing Code (IPC)

13. Which of the following sets the minimum standard of water use reduction?
    a. Energy Policy Act (EPAct) of 1992
    b. Uniform Plumbing Codes (UPC)
    c. WaterSense standards
    d. International Plumbing Code (IPC)

14. The State of California is building a visitor center on a 200,000sf park. How big does the visitor center need to be in order to meet the MPRs for LEED?
    a. 1,000 sf
    b. 2,000 sf
    c. 3,000 sf
    d. 4,000 sf
    e. There is not enough information to determine the minimum sf of the visitor center.

15. What is the maximum number of Regional Priority points a project can achieve?
   a. 3
   b. 4
   c. 5
   d. 6

16. The LEED O&M rating system is different from other LEED rating systems in which of the following ways:
   a. The LEED O&M rating system can be applied to any building type.
   b. The LEED O&M rating system emphasizes measuring and verification.
   c. The LEED O&M rating system emphasizes life cycle costing.
   d. The LEED O&M rating system deals with buildings after construction is completed.

17. Which program is used to qualify off-site green power for LEED?
   a. Green-e
   b. Center for Resource Solution
   c. Green Label
   d. Green Certified

18. Which of the following is the best to measure a material's ability to reflect sunshine?
   a. Albedo
   b. SRI
   c. Color

d. Hue

19. Which of the following will not reduce materials sent to landfill? (Choose 2)
   a. Recycling
   b. Reusing materials
   c. Using regrounded materials
   d. Reducing materials used
   e. Reworking

20. Which of the following will not reduce materials sent to recycling facilities?
   a. Recycling
   b. Reusing materials
   c. Reducing materials used
   d. Reworking

21. Which of the following is the best statement regarding water savings for LEED credits?
   a. Water savings for LEED credits are per building codes.
   b. Water savings for LEED credits are per green building codes.
   c. Water savings for LEED credits are per federal regulations.
   d. Water savings for LEED credits are based on the percentage of water savings achieved by each design case as compared with a baseline building.

22. Which of the following is the best way to alleviate suburban sprawl?
   a. Build more low-rise, high-density housing.
   b. Provide underground parking spaces.
   c. Improve community connectivity.
   d. Provide more pedestrian walkways.

23. A developer has selected an urban site near a shopping center. This will help which of the following?
   a. Community connectivity
   b. Reducing urban runoff
   c. Community relationship
   d. Minimum city code requirements

24. Which of the following is considered open spaces for a LEED project?
   a. Landscape areas
   b. Tennis courts
   c. Sidewalks
   d. Areas under canopy
   e. Atriums with views to the ocean

25. A project seeking LEED certification may incur extra time for the following except:
   a. team member meetings.
   b. a city's plan check.
   c. commissioning.
   d. construction administration.

26. When should a project team start to plan a building's LEED certification?
    a. At schematic design
    b. At design development
    c. At pre-design stage
    d. At construction stage

27. For LEED certification, you should include the following as part of the project's area except:
    a. a parking lot.
    b. a landscape area.
    c. an interior space.
    d. a shared parking structure on a adjacent property.

28. A project team is working on a LEED BDC NC project. How much CFC-refrigerant can the team use?
    a. 2%
    b. 5%
    c. 7%
    d. None

29. Green-e is used for which of the following?
    a. On-site green energy
    b. On-site renewable energy
    c. Off-site renewable energy
    d. None of the above

30. Zero Emission Vehicles (ZEV) are defined by the standards set up by: (Choose 2)
   a. California Air Resources Board
   b. Center for Resource Solution
   c. ACEEE
   d. SCAQMD

31. You are working on a remodel project seeking LEED certification. What should you do about the existing HVAC units containing CFCs?
   a. Replace CFCs with dry ice.
   b. Replace CFCs with natural refrigerant.
   c. Replace CFCs with halons.
   d. Phase out CFCs in 10 years.

32. Which of the following is graywater?
   a. Water from bathroom sinks and kitchen sinks
   b. Water from bathtubs
   c. Water from toilets
   d. Rainwater collected in cisterns
   e. Stormwater that has not come in contract with toilet waste

33. For a building using a halon-based fire suppression system, which of the following is true? (Choose 2)
   a. Halons cause damage to the ozone layer.
   b. This building cannot seek LEED certification.
   c. This building must meet Fire Department

requirements concerning halons.
d. The halons must have a leakage rate of 10% or less.

34. What is the fundamental reason for global warming?
a. Too many cars on the street
b. The use of biofuel
c. Too many green houses were built in the past century
d. Too much Carbon dioxide
e. Too much carbon monoxide

35. SMACNA address which of the following items related to LEED?
a. Metal work
b. VOCs
c. Air quality during construction
d. ODP
e. Certified wood

36. For a project's initial research, what are some of the most important local issues? (Choose 3)
a. Site orientation
b. Parking regulations
c. Incentives for sustainable design
d. ACEEE
e. TRCs

37. Which of the following statements are not true? (Choose 2)
    a. Bicycle racks will help community connectivity.
    b. High SRI pavement will alleviate the heat island effect.
    c. Green roofs can reduce stormwater runoff and alleviate the heat island effect.
    d. Retention ponds will not reduce stormwater runoff.

38. A construction waste management plan should include which of the following?
    a. The recycling capacity of the neighborhood recycle center
    b. Materials to be used for alternative daily cover (ADC)
    c. If the existing ceiling should be reused
    d. The percentage of reused materials

39. A project team is seeking LEED certification for a building. The project can be certified under either the LEED BDC NC or LEED BDC CS rating system. How should the project team determine which LEED system to use? (Choose 2)
    a. Use the system that can gain most points for LEED.
    b. Ask the landlord for advice.
    c. Use the 40/60 rule.
    d. Make an independent decision.
    e. Use the 30/70 rule.

40. A project team is seeking LEED BDC NC certification for a building. Which of the following is true?
    a. The project team cannot seek precertification as a marketing tool for funding and attracting tenants.
    b. The project team can seek precertification as a marketing tool for funding and attracting tenants.
    c. The project must have a signed lease or LOI for at least 70% of the spaces.
    d. The project must be located in a new neighborhood.

41. A project team created a drive-by recycling program for the public to recycle batteries and used electronics. The project team can gain a point under which of the following categories?
    a. SS
    b. MR
    c. IN
    d. EQ

42. What kinds of energy will generate the most pollution? (Choose 3)
    a. Wind
    b. Biofuel
    c. Gas
    d. Natural gas
    e. Nuclear power

43. Which of the following water saving items can be used for outdoor, indoor, and processed water? (Choose 2)
   a. Water efficient fixtures
   b. Sub-meters
   c. Native plants
   d. Water saving education programs

44. Which of the following analyze the potential savings over a building's life span?
   a. ROI
   b. Life-cycle analysis
   c. Life-cycle cost analysis
   d. Life-cycle saving analysis

45. Which of the following includes standards regarding major factors affecting human comfort?
   a. ASHRAE 55-2010
   b. ASHRAE 62.1-2010
   c. Green Label Plus
   d. Green Building Index

46. If you pass the LEED Green Associate Exam, what can you use on your business card?
   a. The GBCI logo
   b. The LEED GA logo per USGBC guidelines
   c. The LEED GA logo per GBCI guidelines
   d. The LEED Green Associate logo per GBCI guidelines
   e. The LEED GA designation only without any logo

47. A tenant purchased some furniture containing VOCs that was manufactured 450 miles from the job site. Which of the following LEED categories will be affected?
   a. SS
   b. EA
   c. MR
   d. EQ
   e. This project cannot seek LEED certification.

48. Green building through a holistic design approach will result in which of the following?
   a. Longer construction time
   b. Shorter construction time
   c. Extra cost
   d. Synergy
   e. Savings over a building's lifetime

49. A project team is seeking LEED certification for an 8-story building. The building has 8 equal floors, and the total square footage of the building is 168,000 sf. What is the building's footprint?
   a. 168,000 sf
   b. 42,000 sf
   c. 21,000 sf
   d. None of the above

50. For the same project mentioned in Question 49, if the total site area is 1 acre, what is the site coverage for this project?

a. 48%
b. 46%
c. 43%
d. 38%

51. For the same project mentioned in Question 49, if the total buildable site area is 1 acre, what is the FAR for this project?
    a. 438%
    b. 386%
    c. 338%
    d. 298%

52. A project team is working on a LEED project composed of 6 buildings on a campus. Each building is located on a 1 acre parcel of land. How should the project team determine the boundary of the LEED project?
    a. Each building should have its own LEED project boundary at the edge of the 1 acre land.
    b. The LEED project boundary should be the perimeter of the 6-acre site.
    c. The project team can make its own decision and determine the LEED project boundary.
    d. There is not enough information to determine the LEED project boundary.

53. A LEED project's landscape area includes which of the following?
   a. Green roofs
   b. Naturalistically designed retention ponds
   c. Sidewalks
   d. Vegetated roofs

54. Which of the following only applies to the LEED EQ category?
   a. ASHRAE Advanced Energy Design Guide for Retail Buildings 2010
   b. ASHRAE Standard 55-2010
   c. ASHRAE 62.1-2010
   d. ASHRAE/IESNA Standard 90.1-2010

55. Which of the following is considered a project soft cost?
   a. Carpet
   b. Doors
   c. Permit Fees
   d. Trees and shrubs

56. Where can a LEED Green Associate find the latest errata for LEED reference guides online?
   a. www.gbci.org
   b. www.nrdc.org
   c. www.usgbc.org
   d. www.epa.gov

57. The heat island effect can typically create ___ degrees Fahrenheit of change in temperature?
   a. 1
   b. 5
   c. 10
   d. 20

58. Who rules on CIRs?
   a. The Technical Advisory Group
   b. The LEED Administrator
   c. GBCI
   d. USGBC

59. Which of the following standards specifies minimum ventilation rates for IAQ Performance?
   a. ASHRAE 52.2-2007
   b. ASHRAE 62.1-2010
   c. ASHRAE/IESNA Standard 90.1-2010
   d. ASTM

60. Who of the following publishes GWP and ODP scores?
   a. The World Meteorological Organization
   b. ASTM
   c. USGBC
   d. The Global Climate Control Board

61. Which of the following are the most commonly used energy codes in the United States?
    a. Universal Energy Conservation Codes
    b. IPC by International Code Council
    c. International Energy Conservation Codes
    d. Energy Rating Codes

62. Which of the following is the most effective way to reduce stormwater runoff?
    a. Building a roof with high SRI value
    b. Using pavers with high albedo
    c. Grouping buildings together
    d. Adding trees to a parking lot

63. Which of the following sites is the best for community connectivity?
    a. A site close to the ocean
    b. A site close to a train station
    c. A brownfield site
    d. A site close to a shopping center

64. Choose the non-alternative-fuel vehicle from the following.
    a. A hybrid car
    b. A bus powered by natural gas with at least 20 mpg
    c. A fuel-efficient car powered by gas with at least 40 mpg
    d. An electric car

65. Which of the following is a car share membership program?
   a. Three or more people going to work in the same vehicle
   b. A program in which two or more people share the cost of a parking space
   c. A shuttle service program from a train station to work places
   d. A program for people to rent a vehicle on a daily or hourly basis

66. Which of the following must be certified under only one LEED rating system?
   a. 100% of the LEED project gross floor area
   b. 80% of the LEED project gross floor area
   c. Everything inside the property boundary
   d. 100% of the LEED project gross site area

67. Which of the following is graywater?
   a. Stormwater
   b. Laundry water
   c. Dishwasher water
   d. Water in retention ponds

68. Which of the following is used to measure a LEED building's environmental performance?
   a. Life cycle analysis
   b. Cradle-to-cradle analysis
   c. Whole building perspective

d. Integrated design approach
e. Overall energy reduction

69. If a LEED project has a CFC phase-out plan, which of the following must occur?
    a. The project can only allow 5% or less of annual CFC leakage.
    b. CFC must be replaced within 15 years.
    c. CFC must be replaced with CO_2.
    d. CFC must be replaced with halons.

70. Which two of the following have the same meaning? (Choose 2)
    a. Albedo
    b. SRI
    c. Refraction
    d. Reflection
    e. Solar Reflectance

71. What are RECs?
    a. The amount of fossil fuels avoided by buying renewable energy and expressed in kilograms
    b. The positive attributes of power generated by renewable sources
    c. The amount of renewable energy purchased from a third party approved by the Green-e program
    d. None of the above

72. The priorities for LEED projects are based on: (Choose 2)
    a. Costs and benefits
    b. Environmental guidelines
    c. Carbon footprint
    d. Project constraints

73. Construction waste reduction strategies include which of the following?
    a. Purchasing materials manufactured locally
    b. Using durable materials
    c. Donating unused materials to charities
    d. Burning the construction waste on site

74. Which of the following is the foundation of the LEED building rating system?
    a. Prerequisites
    b. MPRs
    c. Prerequisites and credits
    d. The triple bottom line

75. A project team is seeking LEED BDC NC certification for a 3-story residential building. Each floor is 600 sf. Which of the following is true?
    a. The project team can seek LEED BDC NC certification because the building is less than 100,000 sf.
    b. The project team can seek LEED BDC NC certification because the building is more than 1,000 sf.
    c. The project team cannot seek LEED

BDC NC certification.
d. The project team can seek LEED BDC NC certification because it meets LEED's MPRs.

76. Per Montreal Protocol, HCFCs have to be phased out by:
   a. 1995
   b. 2010
   c. 2011
   d. 2030

77. If a building's wastewater overflows, which of the following can come into contact with potable water? (Choose 2)
   a. CO
   b. Toxic metal
   c. Grease
   d. Halons

78. The best way to prevent environmental impact caused by refrigerant leakage is to:
   a. Choose high quality plumbing materials, and perform high quality installation and maintenance.
   b. Use refrigerants without ODP.
   c. Design a building with natural ventilation and use no refrigerants.
   d. None of the above

79. A project team is seeking LEED certification for a single building. What does the LEED project boundary include? (Choose 2)
    a. Only the portion of the site submitted by the project team for LEED certification
    b. Overlaps with the edge of the building
    c. Overlaps with the edge of the development
    d. The entire project scope of work

80. The economic benefits of green buildings include: (Choose 2)
    a. Reduced disturbance of wetland
    b. Lower water bills
    c. Increased use of rapidly renewable materials
    d. Better EQ and less liabilities

81. Which of the following is not a fossil fuel? (Choose 2)
    a. Gas
    b. Natural gas
    c. Biofuel
    d. Solar power

82. Which of the following needs to be implemented for water efficiency?
    a. A baseline of water use
    b. HET
    c. Waterless urinals
    d. Xeriscape

83. Which of the following is the most important feature of durability?
    a. The ability to endure and last for a long time
    b. Low maintenance
    c. Little or no unexpected extra costs
    d. Low maintenance and operation expense over the lifetime of the product

84. A project team is preparing a construction waste management plan. Which of the following should be included? (Choose 2)
    a. The removal of refrigerants containing ODP and GWP
    b. Recycle areas
    c. The removal and disposal of hazardous materials like PCBs
    d. The reduction of building size

85. For a LEED project, which of the following should not be used in a fire suppression system? (Choose 2)
    a. Dry ice
    b. Water
    c. HCFCs
    d. CFCs

86. Which of the following can earn points for Innovation? (Choose 2)
   a. Meeting the requirements of all LEED prerequisites and credits
   b. Exceptional performance above and beyond the LEED requirements for an existing credit
   c. Finding a solution responding to the project's regional priorities
   d. Innovative performance in green building categories not covered by an existing LEED credit

87. A project team uses a strategy to earn an Innovation (IN) point for a project in California. Which of the following is true?
   a. The same strategy can be used and guaranteed for an IN point in other projects.
   b. The same strategy can be used for other projects in the same region.
   c. The same strategy may or may not earn an IN point in another project.
   d. None of the above

88. An office building uses ammonia (NH3) as a refrigerant. Which of the following is true?
   a. NH3 has a higher ODP than HCFC.
   b. NH3 has a lower GWP than HCFC.
   c. NH3 is easier to leak out than HCFC.
   d. CFC is easier to leak out than HCFC.

89. A project team is seeking extra points under the Innovation (IN)credit category. Which of

the following is a feasible strategy? (Choose 2)
a. Set up a display area inside the building to educate the public on this building's LEED performance.
b. Try to gain more points than the original target level of LEED certification.
c. Double the performance for a LEED credit.
d. None of the above
e. There is not enough information

90. Which of the following can be the most efficient way to save energy?
a. Proper building orientation and fenestration
b. High performance HVAC systems
c. LEED certified equipment
d. None of the above

91. Which of the following is not true?
a. A LEED project team has to review the USGBC or GBCI website for previously submitted CIRs before submitting a new one.
b. A LEED project team has to review the USGBC reference guide before submitting a CIR.
c. All LEED rating systems can have CIRs except LEED ND.
d. A fee has to be paid for each CIR submitted.

92. ASHRAE standards apply to all of the following except:
    a. SS
    b. WE
    c. EQ
    d. EA

93. Rainwater is:
    a. potable water.
    b. non-potable water.
    c. blackwater.
    d. raw water.
    e. graywater.

94. What are the most important criteria for a LEED building rating system?
    a. Quantifiable performances
    b. Prerequisites
    c. Credits
    d. Third party evaluations
    e. Third party standards

95. Which of the following cannot save water for landscape irrigation? (Choose 2)
    a. Mulches
    b. Perennials
    c. Hardscape
    d. Overhead irrigation
    e. Head to head coverage

96. Energy used by elevators and escalators is:
    a. process energy.
    b. non-process energy.
    c. regulated energy.
    d. renewable energy.
    e. non-renewable energy.

97. Which of the following are most appropriate for a vegetated roof?
    a. Native plants
    b. Trees with large canopies
    c. Adaptive plants
    d. Lightweight plants
    e. There is not enough information to answer this question.

98. Which of the following is a prerequisite for purchasing green power? (Choose 3)
    a. The completion of the commissioning plan
    b. Communication with the key stakeholders
    c. Consultation with an electrical engineer
    d. Compilation of energy data
    e. Evaluation of onsite and offsite energy choices

99. Which of the following is a pre-consumer recycled item?
    a. Aluminum storefront created from materials reclaimed from the manufacturing process
    b. Demolition concrete pieces used at another project
    c. Rigid insulation created from materials reclaimed from the manufacturing process of form cornice
    d. Scraps re-used in the carpet manufacturing process

100. A project team is seeking LEED Platinum certification for a school project. When can the project team advise the school board that the LEED Platinum certification has been achieved?
    a. After the project's substantial completion
    b. After the LEED registration is approved
    c. After the design review
    d. After the construction review
    e. After the LEED application is reviewed and approved by GBCI

II. Answers and Explanations for the LEED Green Associate Mock Exam A

1. Answer: a
   The MEP Engineer has the most influence in energy performance, and the credit, Optimize Energy Performance.

2. Answer: a, c, and e
   The project team should include the following as part of **process energy**:
   Refrigeration and kitchen cooking, laundry (washing and drying), elevators and escalators, computers, office and general miscellaneous equipment, lighting not included in the lighting power allowance (such as lighting that is part of the medical equipment), and other uses like water pumps, etc.

3. Answer: a, c, and d
   The project team should include the following as **regulated (non-process) energy**:
   HVAC, exhaust fans and hoods, lighting for interiors, surface parking, garage parking, building façade and grounds, space heating, and service water heating, etc.

4. Answer: a and b
   Points for the WE category:
   a. LEED BDC NC: 11 points
   b. LEED BDC CS: 11 points
   c. LEED BDC Schools: 12 points
   d. LEED IDC CI: 12 points
   e. LEED OM EB: 12 points

5. Answer: a
   Buildings codes, ADA, Municipal codes, and EPA Codes of Federal Regulations are laws, because they have gone through the legislation process, but reference guides by USGBC are NOT laws. They are rules set by the USGBC and have NO legal authority like the other governing agencies.

   LEED standards are voluntary. You choose to obey the rules when you seek certification for a building, but these rules are NOT laws.

6. Answer: a and c
   The manufacture of HVAC units containing CFCs was stopped in the United States in 1995. These units had been phased out from existing buildings located in the United States by 2011.

7. Answer: c, d, and e
   Increasing the site coverage or FAR will increase impervious area and will increase stormwater runoff. Porous pavement will help recharge the groundwater thereby reducing stormwater runoff, and high-albedo (high-reflectivity) materials will increase reflectivity to alleviate the urban "heat island" effect. Vegetated roofs and retention ponds can also reduce stormwater runoff and alleviate the urban "heat island" effect.

8. Answer: b
   Recycled materials can protect virgin materials, but may require more energy to process, can increase traffic, and increase MEP cost.

9. Answer: f
   Graywater is the household water that has not come into contact with the kitchen sink or toilet waste.

   See USGBC Definitions at the link below:

   https://www.usgbc.org/ShowFile.aspx?DocumentID=5744

   The definitions on the PDF file that you can download from the link above should be read at least three times. Become very familiar with them and MEMORIZE. LEED exams always test these definitions.

10. Answer: c and d
    Blackwater, otherwise known as **brown water**, foul water, or sewage, is water from the kitchen sink, dishwasher, or water that has come into contact with human or animal waste.

11. Answer: a and d
    Read the question carefully; it is asking for the WRONG statements.

12. Answer: b and d
    Both the Uniform Plumbing Code (**UPC**) and International Plumbing Code (**IPC**) set standards for plumbing fixture water use, and their requirements for the water use baseline are the same in many cases.

13. Answer: a
    This question tests your knowledge of the Energy Policy Act (EPAct) of 1992. Although called the Energy Policy Act, it deals with water savings. This is the trick.

14. Answer: d
    MPRs include some very basic requirements. For example:
    1) The building must be 1,000 sf minimum for LEED BDC NC, LEED BDC Schools, LEED BDC CS, and LEED EB: O&M. There is a 250 sf minimum for LEED IDC CI.
    2) The building to site ratio must be 2% or higher. 2% x 200,000 sf = 4,000 sf

15. Answer: b
    The maximum number of Regional Priority points a project can achieve is 4 out of the 6 possible points. A project team needs to select which 4 of the 6 points to use.

16. Answer: d
    The LEED O&M rating system deals with buildings after construction is completed. All

other answers are not unique to LEED O&M.

17. Answer: a
You should use the definition of a renewable source given by the Center for Resource Solution's (CRS) in their Green-e product requirements to determine which power to purchase. The question is asking for a program, not an organization. Center for Resource Solution's (CRS) is an organization, while Green-e is a program.

18. Answer: b
Both albedo and SRI are good indexes, but SRI is the better option. SRI stands for Solar Reflectance Index.

19. Answer: c and e
Pay attention to the word "not" in the question.

20. Answer: a
When you recycle, materials are sent to recycling facilities.

21. Answer: d
LEED is a system set up by USGBC, and not by the federal government or International Code Council (ICC). USGBC is NOT a government agency. Building codes and green building codes are set up by the local government per the ICC model codes.

For LEED, water savings are based on the percentage of water saved by the design case when compared with a baseline building.

22. Answer: c

    Community connectivity is the best answer. The other answers have some merit, but they are not the best answer.

23. Answer: a

    Community connectivity is the best answer. All other answers are distracters to confuse you. If you have a firm knowledge of community connectivity, you should be able to answer this question correctly.

24. Answer: a

    Open spaces need to be vegetated and pervious areas. Areas under canopy and atriums with views to the ocean are typically not considered open spaces for a LEED project.

25. Answer: b

    Pay attention to the word "except" in the question. LEED certification does NOT involve extra time or effort for a city's plan check or permitting.

26. Answer: c

    For planning a project's LEED certification, the earlier this is done in the process, the better.

27. Answer: d

You cannot include a shared parking structure on an adjacent property as part of the project area, because it belongs to someone other than your project owner.

28. Answer: d

You cannot use CFC-refrigerant in new buildings. LEED NC is a rating system for new buildings.

29. Answer: c

Green-e product requirements written by the Center for Resource Solutions are used as guidelines for purchasing your building's electricity from off-site renewable sources. The purchase is based on quantity, NOT the cost, and contracts for this renewable energy should be at least five years long.

30. Answer: a and c

Only vehicles classified as **Zero Emission Vehicles (ZEV)** by California Air Resources Board or vehicles with a green score of at least 45 on the **American Council for an Energy Efficient Economy (ACEEE)** annual vehicle rating guide are qualified as fuel efficient and low emitting vehicles for LEED credit.

31. Answer: b
The manufacture of HVAC units containing CFCs was stopped in the United States in 1995. These units had been phased out from existing U.S. buildings by 2011. Halons are used for fire suppression systems, NOT HVAC systems. Dry ice is commonly used to preserve food, instead of being used as HVAC refrigerant.

32. Answer: b
Per UPC, **graywater** is the household water that has not come into contact with the kitchen sink or toilet waste.

33. Answer: a and c
Halons cause damage to the ozone layer, but a building using a halon-based fire suppression system can still seek LEED certification. This building must meet Fire Department requirements concerning halons.

34. Answer: d
Answers "a" and "b" have some merit, but they are not the fundamental cause of global warming. The rest of the answers are simply distracters.

35. Answer: c
The Sheet Metal and Air Conditioning National Contractors Association (SMACNA) has an IAQ Guideline for Occupied Buildings Under Construction.

36. Answer: a, b, and c
American Council for an Energy Efficient Economy (ACEEE) and Tradable Renewable Certificates (TRCs) are universal and not local issues.

37. Answer: a and d
Please note that we are looking for statements that are <u>NOT</u> true. Bicycle racks will <u>NOT</u> help community connectivity. Retention ponds will reduce stormwater runoff.

38. Answer: b
A construction waste management plan should include materials to be used for alternative daily cover (ADC). Answers "c" and "d" should be part of the design phase decisions. The recycling capacity of the neighborhood recycle center does <u>NOT</u> need to be part of the construction waste management plan.

39. Answer: c and d
Using the system that can gain the most points for LEED makes sense, but is not mandated by USGBC. Asking a landlord for advice is not a good choice and is NOT professional; the project team should be the advisor for the landlord. Using the 40/60 rule is correct. The **40/60 rule for LEED**: if a LEED system applies to 40% or less of the project or spaces, do not use it; if a LEED system applies to 60% or more of the project

or spaces, use it. In the end, the project team makes an independent and final decision.

See "LEED Rating System Selection Policy" at the link below:

http://www.usgbc.org/Docs/Archive/General/Docs10132.pdf

Read this free document at least three times, because it is VERY important, and explains when to use each LEED system.

40. Answer: a
The project team cannot seek precertification as a marketing tool for funding and attracting tenants, because precertification is for the LEED BDC CS (Core and Shell) rating system or LEED Volume Program ONLY. If the project has a signed lease or LOI for at least 70% of the spaces, this is good, but NOT required by GBCI. GBCI also does NOT require the project to be located in a new neighborhood for LEED NC.

41. Answer: c
The project team can gain a point under IN because this program provides quantitative performance improvements for environmental benefit, which is substantially better than typical sustainable practice, and is applicable to other projects. Answer "b" is incorrect because the recycling credit for MR involves

the building occupants (not the general public), and is limited to the following materials only:

> **P**aper
> **C**ardboard
> **M**etal
> **G**lass
> **P**lastics

Mnemonics: People **C**an **M**ake **G**reen **P**romises

42. Answer: c, d, and e
Wind and biofuel are clean energy. Natural gas is pretty clean, but still generates air pollution.

43. Answer: b and d
Using water efficient fixtures applies only to indoor water; using native plants applies only to outdoor water; using sub-meters can monitor water leakage, and applies to all three cases. Water saving education programs can help teach all building users to save water, and applies to all three cases as well.

44. Answer: c
ROI is a return on investment; **life-cycle analysis** is used to analyze the environmental impact of a building over its lifetime; **life-cycle cost analysis** is used to analyze the cost/savings of a building over its lifetime; life-cycle saving analysis is a distracter, and

this term does not exist.

45. Answer: a
    ASHRAE 55-2010 includes standards regarding major factors affecting human comfort, such as temperature, humidity, air speed, etc. **ASHRAE 62.1-2010** is related to natural ventilation; the Carpet and Rug Institute's **Green Label Plus** program is in regard to carpet and rugs; Green Building Index is a sustainable building rating tool used in Malaysia.

46. Answer: d
    If you pass the LEED Green Associate Exam, you can use the LEED Green Associate title or logo per GBCI guidelines on your business card. This question is testing your knowledge about the different scope of work done by GBCI and USGBC, and the proper use of the LEED Green Associate title or logo. Per GBCI, LEED GA is never an approved abbreviation of the LEED Green Associate title or logo.

47. Answer: d
    Furniture containing VOCs will affect EQ. The "450 miles from the job site" is included as a distracter.

48. Answer: d
    Green building through a holistic design ap-

proach has no <u>definite</u> relationship to construction time, cost, or savings over a building's lifetime. The design approach does improve the <u>synergy</u> of LEED credits.

49. Answer: c
The building's foot print = the first-floor area = 168,000 sf/8 = 21,000 sf

50. Answer: a
1 acre = 43,560 sf. The site coverage = the first-floor area/site area = 21,000/43,560= 48%. This question tests your basic construction knowledge: 1 acre = 43,560 sf and the concept of site coverage.

51. Answer: b
FAR (Floor Area Ratio) =the total building area/total **buildable** site area = 168,000/43,560= 386%. This question tests your basic construction knowledge: 1 acre = 43,560 sf.

This question also tests your knowledge of USGBC's definition of FAR which is TOTALLY different from what we are used to in the construction industry. I think this one will throw many people off. It's a good trick.

See USGBC Definitions at the link below:

https://www.usgbc.org/ShowFile.aspx?DocumentID=5744

52. Answer: c
    For a single building project, the perimeter of the LEED project is typically the project's boundary; for a multi-building project, the LEED project team can choose a portion of the project site to submit as the LEED project boundary.

53. Answer: d
    Green roofs include vegetated roofs and light color reflective roofs. Light color reflective roofs are NOT landscape areas. Retention ponds and sidewalks are not considered landscape areas. The best answer is vegetated roofs.

54. Answer: b. ASHRAE Standard 55-2010
    ASHRAE 62.1-2010 relates to both EQ and EA category. The other two standards relate to LEED EA category only.

55. Answer: c
    All the other answers are hard costs (material costs).

56. Answer: c
    USGBC is in charge of creating all reference guides and the related errata.

57. Answer: c
    Pay attention to the word "typically."

58. Answer: a
    Technical Advisory Group is the best answer. The LEED Administrator is a distracter. USGBC is no longer involved with building LEED certification. GBCI depends on the Technical Advisory Group for CIRs.

59. Answer: b
    ASHRAE 62.1-2010 specifies minimum ventilation rates for IAQ Performance. See EAP: Minimum Energy Performance.

60. Answer: a
    ASTM and USGBC do not publish GWP and ODP scores. The Global Climate Control Board does not exist.

61. Answer: c
    Universal Energy Conservation Codes and Energy Rating Codes do not exist. IPC stands for International Plumbing Code.

62. Answer: c
    High SRI value and albedo can help alleviate the heat island effect. Adding trees to a parking lot can reduce stormwater runoff to some extent, but grouping buildings together can reduce the hardscape areas, and is the most effective way to reduce stormwater

runoff.

63. Answer: d
The qualified Basic Services that can help to gain LEED points for community connectivity include, but are not limited to:
a) Place of Worship
b) Restaurant
c) Supermarket
d) Convenience Grocery
e) Laundry
f) Cleaner
g) Beauty Salon
h) Hardware
i) Pharmacy
j) Medical/Dental
k) Bank
l) Senior Care Facility
m) Community Center
n) Fitness Center
o) Daycare
p) School
q) Library
r) Museum
s) Theater
t) Park
u) Fire Station
v) Post Office

A shopping center includes many of the basic services listed above, and is the best choice.

64. Answer: c
A car powered by gas is a non-alternative-fuel vehicle

65. Answer: d
Answer "a" is considered carpooling; Answer "b" is simply sharing parking cost; and Answer "c" is a shuttle service program.

66. Answer: a
A project team does NOT need to certify everything inside the property boundary, and can determine the LEED project site boundary for LEED submittal and certification.

67. Answer: b
Per UPC, **graywater** is household water that has not come into contact with kitchen sinks, human excretion, or animal waste. Graywater includes used water from bathroom washbasins, bathtubs, showers, and water from laundry tubs and clothes washers. Graywater does not include water from dishwashers or kitchen sinks.

68. Answer: c
Cradle-to-cradle analysis is the same as life cycle analysis, eco-balance, or life cycle assessment, and is used to evaluate the environmental impact of a service or product. We use whole building perspective for LEED. Energy reduction is only one aspect of LEED. LEED includes other categories,

such as SS, WE, EQ, etc. Integrated design approach is a design approach that includes consideration for <u>people, planet and profit</u> (triple bottom line or three Ps).

69. Answer: a

CFC can be replaced with CO_2 or other refrigerants. Halons are used for fire suppression systems. The manufacture of HVAC units containing CFCs was stopped in the United States in 1995.These units had been phased out from existing buildings located in the United States by 2011.

70. Answer: a and e

SRI stands for Solar Reflectance Index. Albedo means solar reflectance.

71. Answer: b

RECs mean Renewable Energy Certificates. They represent positive attributes of power generated by renewable sources. When you purchase RECs, you are buying the attributes, NOT necessarily the real power used in your project. Anyone can purchase RECs from anywhere, even if the power used in his/her project is not green power. The money s/he pays allows others to generate or use green power, and achieves overall reduction of the use of fossil fuels in the world. This is a marketing approach for sustainability.

72. Answer: b and d

Per USGBC, the priorities for LEED projects are based on environmental guidelines and project constraints.

73. Answer: c
Burning construction waste on site is not acceptable. Answers "a" and "b" are good practice, but they cannot reduce <u>construction</u> waste.

74. Answer: d
Prerequisites and credits are part of the LEED building rating systems, MPRs are Minimum Project Requirements, and the foundation of the LEED building rating systems is the triple bottom line, which means <u>people, profit, and planet</u>.

75. Answer: c
The project cannot use LEED BDC NC certification because the building is less than 9 stories high. The project team should use the LEED BD+C: Homes and Multifamily Low rise rating system instead.

76. Answer: d
Per Montreal Protocol, the manufacture of HVAC units containing CFCs was stopped in the United States in 1995. These units had been phased out from existing buildings located in the United States by 2011. HCFCs, which are less active, have to be phased out by 2030.

77. Answer: b and c
Grease typically goes down the drains in the kitchen as part of the blackwater. Toxic metal can be found in blackwater also. CO and halons are unlikely to be found in wastewater.

78. Answer: c
Answer "a" is good practice, but is not the best choice; no matter how good a job you do, the system can still fail and leak out refrigerants. Answer "b" is partially correct; there are refrigerants without ODP (ozone depletion potential) that still have GWP (global warming potential). Answer "c" is the best choice; if you do not use refrigerants, there is absolutely no chance for them to leak out and cause environmental damage.

79. Answer: a and d
The LEED project boundary only includes the portion of the site submitted by the project team for LEED certification, and does not necessarily overlap with the edge of the entire development, or the edge of the building. The boundary does include the entire project scope of work

80. Answer: b and d
Reduced disturbance of wetlands is an envi-

ronmental benefit, not necessarily an economic benefit. Increased use of rapidly renewable materials may not save money. Better EQ does create fewer liabilities, lowers the cost related to employees' health, and reduces the number of employee sick days.

81. Answer: c and d
Biofuel is generated from plant material like crops, trees, and grasses. Gas and natural gas are both fossil fuels.

82. Answer: a
All other choices are good practice, but they do NOT necessarily need to be implemented for water efficiency.

83. Answer: a
This is the definition of durability.

84. Answer: b and c
The removal of refrigerants containing ODP and GWP should be conducted by a specialist, and is not part of a construction waste management plan. The reduction of building size is part of the design decision, not part of a construction waste management plan.

85. Answer: c and d
HCFCS and CFCs should not be used because of their ozone depletion potential (ODP).

86. Answer: b and d
Both answer "b" and "d" can earn points for Innovation.

87. Answer: c
The same strategy can be used for other projects, but it may or may not earn an IN point. Each case has to be reviewed and determined by GBCI.

88. Answer: b
NH3 has a lower GWP than HCFC.

For more information see: "**The Treatment by LEED of the Environmental Impact of HVAC Refrigerants**." You can download this PDF file for free at the link below:

http://www.gbci.org/Files/References/The-Treatment-by-LEED-of-the-Environmental-Impact-of-HVAC-Refrigerants.pdf

This is a VERY important document that you need to become familiar with. Many real LEED exam questions (CFC, HCFC, HFC, etc.) come from this document. You should download the file and read at least 3 times.

Pay special attention to the Table on ODP and GWP. You do not have to remember the exact value of all ODPs and GWPs, but you do need to know the rough number for various groups of refrigerants.

89. Answer: a and c
An educational program on LEED is the most common way to gain points under the Innovation category. Answer "c" may earn extra points for Exemplary Performance under the Innovation category. Answer "b" may help the project earn a higher level of LEED certification, but no other rewards.

90. Answer: a
Proper building orientation and fenestration can take full advantage of the dominant winds in the summer, and avoid chilly north winds in the winter. These characteristics can also take full advantage of passive heating from the sun in the winter, and avoid the westerly sun in the summer. This can be more efficient than ALL the HVAC equipment combined. There is no such thing as LEED certified equipment.

91. Answer: c
All LEED rating systems can have CIRs, including LEED ND.

92. Answer: b
ASHRAE standards do not apply to WE.

93. Answer: b
Rainwater is non-potable water. Please also see the definitions for blackwater and graywater in the explanations of Questions #9,

#10, #32, and #67. Raw water is a distracter.

94. Answer: b
Prerequisites are the most important criteria for a LEED building rating system. They *have to* be met before a building can earn LEED certification. Quantifiable performances, credits, and third-party standards only apply to part of the LEED rating systems, and not ALL of them have to be met.

95. Answer: b and d
Hardscape can reduce landscape area; mulches can prevent moisture loss. Both can reduce water for landscape irrigation. Perennials use more water. Overhead irrigation can increase water loss due to runoff and evaporation by the sun and wind. Head to head coverage is a standard practice for landscape irrigation.

96. Answer: a
Energy used by elevators and escalators is process energy and can be renewable energy or non-renewable energy. Non-process energy is the same as regulated energy.

The energy used by the following is considered **process energy**:
Refrigeration and kitchen cooking, laundry (washing and drying), elevators and escalators, computers, office and general miscellaneous equipment, lighting not included in the

lighting power allowance (such as lighting that is part of the medical equipment), and other uses like water pumps, etc.

The energy used by the following is considered **regulated (non-process) energy**: HVAC, exhaust fans and hood, lighting for interiors, surface parking, garage parking, building façade and grounds, space heating and service water heating, etc.

97. Answer: d
Lightweight plants are most appropriate for a vegetated roof. Native plants or adaptive plants are good for LEED projects, but some of them are NOT appropriate for rooftops. A native tree with a large canopy on a vegetated roof means large roots will be present and may cause many problems.

98. Answer: b, d, and e
Consultation with an electrical engineer is good practice, but it is not as important as the other choices. The completion of the commissioning plan will occur AFTER on-site renewable systems are selected.

99. Answer: c
Scraps re-used from the same manufacture process, such as reground and rework, cannot be included as pre-consumer recycled items or post-consumer recycled items.

Therefore, Answers "a" and "d" are incorrect. Demolition concrete pieces used at another project are salvaged materials.

100. Answer: e
    The project team can ONLY advise the school board that the LEED Platinum certification is achieved after the LEED application is reviewed and APPROVED by GBCI, because the GBCI can reject the application after the review or approve the project for a lower level of LEED certification.

Chapter 2
LEED GREEN ASSOCIATE Mock Exam B:
Questions, Answers, and Explanations

I. Important Note: Read this before you work on LEED GREEN ASSOCIATE Mock Exam B

1. **How much time should you spend on preparing for the LEED exam?**

   Answer: Some people spend too much time preparing for the LEED exam, and by the time they take the real test, they may have forgotten a lot of the information already.

   Timing is VERY critical. If you pass the practice test with a score of 190 three months before the real test, by the time you take the test, you may have forgotten the information and score much lower.

   One way to overcome this is NOT to take too

much time to prepare for the LEED exam, and save at least one mock exam to use in the last week before the exam. You should NOT read any questions on this reserved mock exam until one or two weeks before the exam. This way, you can alert and energize yourself one more time right before the real exam, and work on your weaknesses. You can save the LEED GREEN ASSOCIATE Mock Exam B for this purpose.

There is one reader who passed the LEED Green Associate Exam by studying my two books, *LEED Green Associate Exam Guide* and *LEED GREEN ASSOCIATE Mock Exam,* for 10 hours in total.

For an average reader, I recommend not less than 2 weeks, but not MORE than 2 months of prep time. If you read *LEED Green Associate Exam Guide*, you'll understand why too much prep time may hurt your chance of passing the exam.

II. LEED GREEN ASSOCIATE Mock Exam B

101. A project team decides to phase out some of the existing HVAC units that have CFC-based refrigerants. What is the maximum allowable annual refrigerant leakage rate?
    a. 0%
    b. 2%

c. 5%
d. 10%

102. Which of the following are must-have feature of open spaces? (Choose 2)
    a. Vegetation
    b. Shade
    c. Brownfields
    d. Pervious Areas
    e. Hardscape Areas

103. Which of the following is true regarding HCFC-22?
    a. The refrigerant has a high GWP and high ODP.
    b. The refrigerant has a high GWP and low ODP.
    c. The refrigerant has a low GWP and high ODP.
    d. The refrigerant has a low GWP and low ODP.

104. A LEED certified building has the following extra costs when compared with a conventional building?
    a. Hard costs
    b. Soft costs
    c. Storm control costs
    d. Life cycle analysis costs
    e. Life cycle cost analysis

105. Per USGBC, an average commercial building can achieve which of the following percentage of water savings without extra costs?
   a. 5%
   b. 10%
   c. 20%
   d. 30%
   e. 40%

106. Where in the USGBC reference guide can a project team find special information for a region?
   a. A Genius Loci
   b. Regional Priority
   c. Resources
   d. Further reference

107. Which of the following specializes in evaluating the energy performance of different buildings?
   a. LEED
   b. LEED scores
   c. Levels of LEED certification
   d. Energy Star
   e. RECs

108. A project team can earn extra credits for which of the following? (Choose 2)
   a. Exceeding minimum project requirements
   b. Innovative performance in green building categories not covered by an existing LEED credit.

c. Having three principal participants of the project team who are a LEED Accredited Professional (AP) with a specialty appropriate for the project.
d. Meeting all prerequisites and some critical credits

109. The Green-e program applies to which of the following LEED categories?
a. SS
b. WE
c. EA
d. EQ

110. All LEED rating systems include credits for:
a. emission measurement.
b. radon alleviation.
c. minimum energy performance.
d. innovation.

111. Which of the following is not true?
a. A project earning IN points will need to be followed up after 18 months to verify that the strategy is working.
b. IN points are awarded for exemplary performance in categories not covered by an existing LEED credit.
c. A creative strategy addressing environmental issues specific to the project's region can earn IN points.
d. An education program could earn IN points.

112. Which of the following have the lowest ODP?
    a. CFCs
    b. HCFCs
    c. HFCs
    d. This is hard to determine.

113. A project has earned 81 LEED points under LEED v4. What level of LEED certification has the project achieved?
    a. LEED Platinum Certified
    b. LEED Gold Certified
    c. LEED Platinum
    d. LEED Silver
    e. LEED Bronze
    f. LEED Certified

114. On average, what percentage of energy do green buildings save when compared with conventional buildings?
    a. About 10%
    b. About 15%
    c. About 20%
    d. About 25%

115. Which part of the process uses proper design material, selection, and construction practices to promote high performance and durability of the building envelope, components, and systems?
    a. Durability management verification
    b. Design charrettes
    c. LEED charrettes
    d. Material selection

116. The baseline water use for a kitchen sink is?
    a. 2.0 gpm at 60 psi
    b. 2.2 gpm at 60 psi
    c. 2.0 gpm at 80 psi
    d. 2.2 gpm at 80 psi

117. Choose the post-consumer item from the following.
    a. Construction debris sent to a recycle facility
    b. Scraps from a manufacturing process
    c. Books from a print overrun
    d. Scraps from a manufacturing process that were reclaimed and used in a different manufacturing process

118. Which of the following is true?
    a. Starting on January 1, 2010, CFCs are no longer used in the United States.
    b. CFCs have no ODP.
    c. There is no ideal substitute for CFCs.
    d. EPA has no control over CFCs.

119. Which of the following evaluates the environmental performance of services and products?
   a. ASTM
   b. ISO 14000
   c. ANSI
   d. LEED

120. Which of the following occupancy rates are required for a project to qualify for the LEED O&M rating system?
   a. The normal physical occupancy rate for a similar building
   b. 60%
   c. 80%
   d. None of the above

121. A major renovation of an existing retail building can use which LEED rating systems? (Choose 2)
   a. LEED O&M for existing buildings
   b. LEED BDC NC
   c. LEED BDC CS
   d. LEED ND

122. Which of the following is true regarding used water from a bathroom sink?
   a. The water cannot be reused.
   b. The water is graywater and can always be reused.
   c. The water may be reused if acceptable per local codes.
   d. None of the above

123. Which of the following is true regarding Regional Priority points?
   a. They encourage the use of regional materials.
   b. They encourage the use of regional materials within 100 miles of the project site.
   c. They are related to the project's zip code.
   d. They encourage the use of regional materials manufactured within 100 miles of the project.

124. A tenant leases an 8,000-sf space from a 12,000-sf office building. Which of the following is true? (Choose 2)
   a. This building cannot seek LEED O&M certification.
   b. This building can seek LEED O&M certification.
   c. The tenant can seek LEED O&M certification for his space.
   d. This building needs to be recertified periodically.

125. Which of the following is true regarding local ordinances?
   a. They are typically part of municipal codes.
   b. They are a local adaptation of the national model codes.
   c. They are local regulations enforced to

prevent land use conflicts.
d. None of the above

126. Which of the following should never be included as local materials?
   a. HVAC units
   b. Tables and chairs
   c. Carpet
   d. Concrete

127. Which of the following can help to alleviate the heat island effect?
   a. Planting trees to provide shade for open spaces
   b. Providing the minimum number of parking spaces required by codes
   c. Using open grid pavers
   d. Placing mulch around the landscape area

128. Which of the following is not true? (Choose 2)
   a. A project team can hire a LEED AP with a specialty appropriate for the project as a consultant to support the LEED project.
   b. A LEEDCI project has to have a LEED AP ID+C as a principal in the team.
   c. Each project enrolled in the USGBC's portfolio program requires a LEED AP with a specialty appropriate for the project on the team.
   d. A project can earn LEED certification

without having a LEED AP as a principal in the team.

129. What is FAR?
    a. The area of the building footprint divided by the total site area
    b. The area of the building footprint divided by the total buildable site area
    c. The total area of all the floors of the building divided by the total site area
    d. The total area of all the floors of the building divided by the total buildable site area

130. Which of the following includes a proposed requirement as part of the submittal?
    a. IN credit submittal
    b. Energy baseline submittal
    c. Water baseline submittal
    d. Waste management plan submittal
    e. CFC phase-out plan submittal

131. Which of the following should not be placed into a comingled recycle box? (Choose 2)
    a. Light bulbs
    b. Batteries
    c. Cardboard
    d. Plastics
    e. Metal

132. Which of the following is an important consideration for the recycle area?
   a. An enclosure made of durable materials like CMU
   b. Inclusion of an area for balers
   c. Inclusion of an area for can crushers
   d. Easy accessibility
   e. Inclusion of an area for hazardous materials

133. A project team is trying to earn an IN point by designating an area on the first floor of a multi-story building to display educational materials about the project's LEED credits. Which of the following is true?
   a. If the project team can earn one IN point for this project, they will also earn one IN point for another project because LEED IN points are transferable.
   b. If the project team can earn one IN point for this project, they will also earn one IN point for another project only if the other project is also a multi-story building.
   c. The display area needs to be accessible to all occupants of the building to qualify for one IN point.
   d. The display area needs to include information about every LEED credit awarded to the building in order to qualify for one IN point.

134. Which of the following is the lowest level of LEED certification?
   a. LEED bronze
   b. LEED certified
   c. LEED silver
   d. LEED Certified
   e. LEED gold

135. Which of the following do not contribute to the heat island effect? (Choose 2)
   a. Car exhaust
   b. High-albedo pavement
   c. HVAC equipment
   d. Bio-retention ponds

136. Which of the following should be used to wash dishes?
   a. Portable water
   b. Stormwater
   c. Water from bio-retention ponds
   d. Potable water
   e. Graywater
   f. Blackwater

137. If the LEED project administrator adds Mike, a team member, to LEED Online, Mike can: (Choose 2)
   a. Download a PDF format of the USGBC reference guide after he logs into LEED Online
   b. Submit CIRs
   c. Use LEED Online to do research and search through materials for the LEED

project
d. Find out which credits have been approved, including the ones he is not working on

138. A school project is reusing some old furniture from an office building 120 miles away from the project site. Which credit will this decision help the project to earn? (Choose 2)
    a. Recycled content
    b. Building Life-Cycle Impact Reduction
    c. Regional materials
    d. Construction and Demolition Waste Management Planning

139. A developer decides to plant trees along the edge of a parking lot, which of the following is a benefit of this decision?
    a. Alleviation of heat island effect
    b. Lower maintenance costs
    c. Better IAQ
    d. Reduction of stormwater runoff

140. Which of the following is true regarding refrigerants? (Choose 2)
    a. A refrigerant with low ODP often has high GWP, with HFC as an exception.
    b. A refrigerant with low ODP often has low GWP, with HFC as an exception.
    c. A refrigerant with high ODP often has low GWP, with HFC as an exception.
    d. A refrigerant with high ODP often has high GWP, with HFC as an exception.

141. An engineer is not sure if a particular modeling software can be used for measuring energy performance of a LEED credit, what should s/he do?
   a. Submit a RFI to the LEED administrator.
   b. Submit a CIR to the USGBC task force.
   c. Submit a CIR via LEED Online.
   d. Submit a CIR through LEED Online only if the credit is denied.

142. Which of the following will maximize open spaces?
   a. Building on a greenfield
   b. Building on a brownfield
   c. Building on a previously developed site
   d. Building a 12-story building instead of a 6-story building

143. Which of the following use CFCs? (Choose 2)
   a. Garbage disposals
   b. Refrigeration
   c. Humidifiers
   d. Recycling

144. Which of the following are the most important issues to a project team?
   a. Building department requirements
   b. Zoning requirements
   c. Parks nearby
   d. Pedestrian access

145. A project team has completed the LEED scorecard, what should they do with it?
a. Refer to it during construction.
b. Fax it to GBCI.
c. Submit it via LEED Online.
d. Use it to determine the LEED consultation cost.

146. Which of the following is not a goal for MPRs?
a. To provide clear guidance for customers
b. To maintain LEED program integrity
c. To set up minimum environmental goals
d. To make the LEED certification process easier

147. Which of the following are not natural refrigerants? (Choose 3)
a. CO
b. CO_2
c. NH_3
d. Propane
e. Halons
f. Radon

148. Which of the following has the least ODP?
a. CFC
b. HCFH
c. CO_2
d. HFC

149. A project team is designing a school project in a remote area of China. Because of the local conditions, they decide to use mud within 5 miles of the project site to build a 3-foot-thick wall instead of using insulation. Which of the following is true? (Choose 3)
   a. This project cannot achieve LEED certification because it is outside of the United States.
   b. This project can achieve LEED certification even though it is outside of the United States.
   c. The project team's decision can help the project earn points for Regional Materials.
   d. The project team's decision can help the project earn points for reducing the heat island effect.
   e. The project team's decision can reduce the energy cost of the building.

150. Which of the following is the most important for energy savings?
   a. Proper building orientation
   b. Efficient HVAC equipment
   c. Operable windows
   d. Sun shading devices

151. Which of the following cannot help a project team earn LEED points for reducing the heat island effect? (Choose 2)
    a. Providing light colored shading devices
    b. Using adaptive plants
    c. Placing parking underground
    d. Providing shuttle service to bus stations

152. A project team is seeking LEED certification for a building. To gain one point for open space, the open space of this project needs to be:
    a. 50% of the project site area minus the building footprint.
    b. 30% of the project site area minus the development footprint.
    c. 50% the project site area (including the building footprint), and the open space can include retention ponds.
    d. 30% the project site area (including the building footprint), and the open space must be vegetated and pervious.

153. A manufacturer's representative can make the following claims about a wood product? (Choose 2)
    a. The product is LEED certified.
    b. The product meets all the requirements of FSC.
    c. The product meets the requirements of Environmental Product Declarations.
    d. The product contributes to meeting the requirements of Environmental Product

Declarations under the LEED building rating system.

154. Which of the following is true?
   a. Ozone does not have negative environmental impacts. That is why we promote the use of products with low ODP (ozone depletion potential).
   b. Ozone located at the upper atmosphere has negative environmental impacts.
   c. Ozone can have negative or positive environmental impacts, depending on where it is located.
   d. Ozone located at the lower atmosphere has positive environmental impacts.

155. A project saves 55% of landscape irrigation water when compared with the baseline. Under which LEED credit or credit category will the project earn exemplary points?
   a. WE category
   b. WE Credit (WEC): Outdoor Water Use Reduction
   c. WEC: Indoor Water Use Reduction
   d. Innovation credit

156. Which of the following uses the most energy in a building?
   a. Ventilation
   b. Space heating
   c. Cooling
   d. Lighting

157. Which of the following has the lowest priority?
   a. LEED standards
   b. Mechanical codes
   c. Zoning requirements
   d. Building codes

158. Which of the following is the project boundary?
   a. The platted property line of the project
   b. The area within the legal property line of the project
   c. The area within the legal property line of the project submitted to GBCI for LEED certification
   d. The area within the legal property line of the project, excluding non-buildable area

159. Greenfield means:
   a. a park.
   b. a contaminated site.
   c. a habitat.
   d. a previously developed site.
   e. a previously undeveloped site.
   f. farmland.

160. A LEED project team is working on an existing building with existing HVAC&R units that use CFC-based refrigerants. Which of the following is true? (Choose 2)
   a. This project cannot earn LEED certification.
   b. The project team needs to replace all

HVAC&R units with new ones.
c. The project team can choose to phase out the CFC-based refrigerants before the project completion.
d. The project team can choose to phase out the CFC-based refrigerants after the project completion as long as the phase out plan is approved by the GBCI.
e. The project team can choose to phase out the CFC-based refrigerants within 15 years of the project completion as long as the refrigerant leakage rate is 5% or less.

161. Which of the following is true?
a. The Clean Air Act requires that no importation or production of HCFCs in the United States will be allowed after 2030.
b. The Clean Air Act requires the use of low emission vehicles to alleviate air pollution.
c. The Clean Air Act set up standards to control air-borne dust that occurs during construction.
d. The Clean Air Act requires that no importation or production of HCFCs in the United States are allowed after 2011.

162. What percentage of garbage in U.S. landfills comes from demolition and construction debris?
   a. 30%
   b. 40%
   c. 50%
   d. 60%

163. What is the difference between life cycle costing (LCC) and life cycle assessment (LCA)?
   a. LCA focuses on economic analysis while LCC focuses on environmental analysis.
   b. LCC focuses on economic analysis while LCA focuses on environmental analysis.
   c. LCA focuses on environmental and economic analysis.
   d. LCC focuses on environmental and economic analysis.

164. With regard to refrigerants, what is the dilemma between ODP and GWP?
   a. Refrigerants have ODP.
   b. Refrigerants with high ODP are less efficient.
   c. Refrigerants with neutral ODP are less efficient.
   d. Refrigerants with high ODP have high GWP.

165. A project team develops a new way to achieve reduction of the heat island effect. What extra LEED point can the team earn?
   a. One Exceptional performance point
   b. One Innovative performance point
   c. One bonus point under the heat island effect
   d. Zero extra points will be awarded

166. What percentage of water chillers in existing U.S. buildings still used CFCs in 2009?
   a. 20%
   b. 30%
   c. 40%
   d. 50%

167. Drawing a circle with a ½ mile radius around the project site will help the project team to determine which of the following?
   a. Distance to basic services
   b. Distance to public transit
   c. Distance to water services
   d. None of the above

168. A project team is seeking LEED certification for an existing building. Which of the following can be used to replace CFC-based refrigerants? (Choose 2)
   a. Natural refrigerants only
   b. HFCs and HCFCs only
   c. Natural ventilation
   d. Natural refrigerants and HCFCs
   e. Any non-CFC-based refrigerants

169. A contractor demolishes the interior partition of an office building, and recycles the construction debris and waste. S/he also reuses the exterior building shell. S/he can earn LEED points for which of the following credits? (Choose 2)
   a. Regional materials
   b. Recycled content
   c. Building reuse
   d. Construction waste management

170. A project team intends to seek bonus points for two credits. Which of the following is true?
   a. The project team has to submit CIRs for these two credits.
   b. The project team has to pay an extra fee for each of the bonus points.
   c. A LEED AP with a specialty appropriate for the project has to submit these two credits via LEED Online.
   d. These two credits have to be submitted for final review by the Project Administrator.

171. Which of the following is used to draw on the expertise of all LEED team members?
   a. Pre-bid meeting
   b. Design charrettes
   c. LEED Technical Advisory Group
   d. Brainstorm meeting

172. Which of the following LEED categories can award LEED points for renewable energy production? (Choose 2)
    a. SS
    b. WE
    c. EA
    d. EQ
    e. IN

173. A building program that details the project's green building requirements does not include: (Choose 2)
    a. The green building goals
    b. The project's vision
    c. A general description of the project
    d. A room-by-room description of the project
    e. Construction cost
    f. Scope of work

174. A density radius calculation is used for:
    a. calculating the number of basic services included for the LEED credit.
    b. calculating the number of amenities included for the LEED credit.
    c. calculating the number of public transit locations included for the LEED credit.
    d. determining the number of properties included in the Surrounding Density and Diverse Uses calculation.

175. On average, what percentage of potable water is used for landscape irrigation in the US?
   a. 20%
   b. 30%
   c. 40%
   d. 50%

176. Which of the following will reduce the number of solo drivers? (Choose 2)
   a. A shortage of parking spaces
   b. Incentive for carpooling
   c. Locating the project close to downtown
   d. Increasing FAR

177. For a project seeking LEED certification, which of the following is not a strategy to reduce environmental impact from refrigerants?
   a. Using refrigerants with low ODP and GWP
   b. Using propane instead of CFC-based refrigerants
   c. Reducing the annual leakage rate of the refrigerants to 10% or less
   d. Using natural refrigerants

178. The USGBC and LEED were created to:
   a. provide a platform for all green building organizations to interact.
   b. provide a measurement and verification for green buildings.
   c. provide a system to define and measure

green building.
d. provide an organization and system to spread green building information.

179. Which of the following is not related to EQ category? (Choose 2)
a. TARP
b. Green Label Plus
c. Green-e
d. SMACNA
e. Agrifiber Products

180. During construction, a project team should use filtration media with a Minimum Efficiency Reporting Value (MERV) of _ at each return air grille per ASHRAE 52.2-2007.
a. 6
b. 8
c. 13
d. 15

181. Which of the following is related to Construction IAQ Management Plan?
a. ASHRAE 52.2-2007
b. ASHRAE Standard 55-2010
c. ASHRAE 62.1-2010
d. ASHRAE/IESNA Standard 90.1-2010

182. Which of the following is related to ventilation?
   a. ASHRAE 52.2-2007
   b. ASHRAE Standard 55-2010
   c. ASHRAE 62.1-2010
   d. ASHRAE/IESNA Standard 90.1-2010

183. Which of the following is related to thermal comfort?
   a. ASHRAE 52.2-2007
   b. ASHRAE Standard 55-2010
   c. ASHRAE 62.1-2010
   d. ASHRAE/IESNA Standard 90.1-2010

184. Which of the following could be the life cycle costing benefits of a vegetated roof?
   a. Lower overall costs
   b. Reduced heat island effect
   c. Savings in landscape irrigation costs
   d. Extra outdoor activities areas for building users

185. The USGBC logo can be used by:
   a. organizations approved by USGBC.
   b. USGBC members.
   c. LEED Green Associate.
   d. LEED APs with a specialty.
   e. USGBC Chapters.

186. Which of the following is true concerning CIRs?
   a. CIRs cannot be submitted before precertification.
   b. CIRs cannot be submitted before design submittal.
   c. A LEED project team should submit CIRs that have been ruled on with the LEED application.
   d. CIRs cannot be submitted before construction stage.

187. Which of the following has the least impact on a project's landscape design?
   a. CC&R
   b. Zoning Ordinances
   c. EPAct
   d. Building codes

188. Which of the following is not a benefit of Integrated Project Delivery (IPD)?
   a. Optimal project results
   b. Increased value to the owner
   c. Integrated financial performance for all participants
   d. Reduced waste

189. One issue with bioenergy is:
   a. that most people have not accepted its concept.
   b. the amount of fossil fuel energy used in its production.
   c. that it has not been approved by USGBC
   d. that it will not contribute to LEED credit.

190. Biomass is _____ converted to heat energy to produce electricity.
   a. plant material
   b. animal waste
   c. underground organic materials
   d. underground sediment

191. For a LEED BDC NC project to gain one LEED point, a project team needs to provide views (direct line of sight to the outside) for __ of all regularly occupied spaces.
   a. 66%
   b. 75%
   c. 85%
   d. 95%

192. For a LEED BDC NC project, an area needs to have two of the following kinds of approved views including the except:
   a. unobstructed views located within the distance of four times the head height of the vision glazing
   b. views with a view factor of 3 or greater
   c. multiple lines of sight to vision glazing in different directions at least 90 degrees apart
   d. views that include at least two of the following: (1) flora, fauna, or sky; (2) movement; and (3) objects at least 25 feet (7.5 meters) from the exterior of the glazing

193. Which of the following is not related to IAQ?
   a. Light bulbs
   b. Furniture
   c. Carpet
   d. Paint

194. For a LEED School project, how many points can a project team earn under Minimum IAQ Performance?
   a. 0
   b. 1
   c. 2
   d. 3

195. Which of the following can help a LEED BDC NC project earn one point?
   a. Giving individual thermal comfort controls for at least 40% of individual occupant spaces. Provide group thermal comfort controls for at least 80% of shared multi-occupant spaces.
   b. Giving individual thermal comfort controls for at least 50% of individual occupant spaces. Provide group thermal comfort controls for at least 80% of shared multi-occupant spaces.
   c. Giving individual thermal comfort controls for at least 40% of individual occupant spaces. Provide group thermal comfort controls for all shared multi-occupant spaces.
   d. Giving individual thermal comfort controls for at least 50% of individual occupant spaces. Provide group thermal comfort controls for all shared multi-occupant spaces.

196. To minimize building users' exposure to chemical pollutants and possibly dangerous particulates, a project team should provide hard lid ceilings, deck-to-deck partitions, and self-closing doors for the following spaces except:
   a. copying/printing rooms.
   b. laundry/housekeeping areas.
   c. gift shops.

d. art rooms.

197. Using composite wood and agrifiber products can affect which of the following LEED credit categories? (Choose 2)
    a. SS
    b. MR
    c. EA
    d. EQ

198. For LEED BDC CS, which of the following standards are related to EQ category? (Choose 2)
    a. SCAQMD
    b. Green Seal Standard
    c. Green-e
    d. Green Label Plus

199. Which of the following are related to Light Pollution Reduction? (Choose 2)
    a. BUG
    b. LUG
    c. MLO
    d. MLH

200. Building orientation can contribute to the following except:
    a. optimizing energy performance.
    b. green power.
    c. better natural ventilation.
    d. passive solar heating.

III. Answers and Explanations for the LEED GREEN ASSOCIATE Mock Exam B

101. Answer: c

102. Answer: a and d
Open spaces must be pervious and vegetated. They are non-built environments.

103. Answer: b
HCFC-22 has a high GWP and low ODP. See the free PDF file, "The Treatment by LEED of the Environmental Impact of HVAC Refrigerants," for more information.

104. Answer: e
Life cycle cost analysis is unique to a LEED certified building. Hard costs, soft costs, and storm control costs are required by both a LEED certified building and a conventional building. Life cycle analysis costs is different from life cycle cost analysis, and is a distracter.

Life cycle cost analysis is an evaluation of a building's economic performance including operational and maintenance costs over the life of the product.

Life cycle analysis is the same as eco-balance, cradle-to-cradle analysis, or life cycle assessment. It is used to evaluate the environmental impact of a service or product.

105. Answer: d

106. Answer: b
See the LEED reference guides for more information.

A **Genius Loci** was the protective spirit of a place in classical Roman religion. It is a term used in architecture.

107. Answer: d
Energy Star specializes in energy performance. LEED includes energy performance and other criteria. RECs are the positive attributes of power generated by renewable sources.

108. Answer: b and c
A project team can earn extra credits for:
1) Innovative performance in green building categories not covered by an existing LEED credit
2) Having at least one principal participant of the project team who is a LEED Accredited Professional (AP) with a specialty appropriate for the project

Meeting all prerequisites and some critical credits or exceeding minimum project requirements may earn LEED certification for the project, but may not earn extra credits.

109. Answer: c

    The Green-e Program applies to the LEED EA category.

110. Answer: d

    Minimum energy performance is a prerequisite, not a credit. Emission measurement and radon alleviation are distracters.

111. Answer: a

    A project earning IN points does NOT need to be followed up after 18 months to verify that the strategy is working.

112. Answer: c

    Concerning ozone depletion potential (ODP): CFCs>HCFCs>HFCs. Therefore, HFCs have the lowest ODP.

113. Answer: c

    LEED Platinum Certified is not a proper term. LEED Platinum is the correct term.

No matter which **LEED v4** rating system you choose, each LEED v4 rating system has **100**base points, a maximum of **6** possible extra points for Innovation, and a maximum of **4** possible extra points for Regional Priority (RP) for each project. There are 6 possible RP points, but you can only pick and choose a maximum of 4 points for each project.

Chapter 2: Mock Exam B•117

Certified	**40**–49	points
Silver	**50**–59	points
Gold	**60**–79	points
Platinum	**80**	points and above

114. Answer: d
This is based on a study undertaken by the New Buildings Institute.

115. Answer: a
This is the intent of the durability management verification for the LEED Homes rating system

116. Answer: b
See the Flow Rates Table under the WE category of *LEED Green Associate Exam Guide*. This table is VERY important. You ABSOLUTELY need to **memorize** the **numbers** on this table. Every LEED exam will test this information.

117. Answer: a
Construction debris sent to a recycle facility is the only item that has been used by a consumer, and is therefore a post-consumer item.

118. Answer: c
CFCs were still used in some existing U.S. buildings until 2011.

119. Answer: b

ISO 14000 evaluates the environmental performance of services and products. It includes Design for Environment, Life Cycle Assessment, and Environmental Labels and Declaration.

120. Answer: a

A building needs to have the normal physical occupancy rate of a similar building to qualify for the LEED O&M rating system. For example, a brand-new office building does NOT qualify for the LEED O&M rating system, but if after 1 year, the building has the normal physical occupancy rate for a similar office building, it will qualify.

121. Answer: b and c

LEED O&M for existing buildings deals with operation and maintenance. LEED ND is for neighborhood development.

122. Answer: c

Used water from a bathroom sink may be reused for landscape irrigation or flushing toilets, if acceptable per local codes

123. Answer: c

All other choices are related to the MR category instead of the RP category. They are distracters.

124. Answer: b and d
This whole building (NOT individual tenant spaces within the building) can seek LEED O&M certification, and needs to be recertified periodically (at least every 5 years).

125. Answer: a
Local ordinances are typically part of municipal codes. Answer "b" is regarding local codes. Answer "c" is in regard to zoning codes.

126. Answer: a
Do not include electrical, mechanical, and plumbing items, elevators and equipment, or other specialty items in your calculation of regional or local materials. You can only include permanently installed materials for your job. You can include furniture (Answer "b") only if it is consistently included in other related MR credits. Pay attention to the word "**never**" in the question.

127. Answer: c
Answer "a" is incorrect because open spaces are vegetated and pervious areas. Planting trees to provide shade for open spaces will NOT alleviate the heat island effect. Using open grid pavers will allow vegetation to grow inside the open grid and can help to alleviate the heat island effect.

128. Answer: b and c
Currently all LEED projects need to have a LEED AP with a specialty appropriate for the project as a principal in the team to earn one IN point. However, each project enrolled in the USGBC's portfolio program does NOT require a LEED AP with a specialty appropriate for the project on the team.

129. Answer: d
FAR is Floor Area Ratio, and is defined as the total area of all the floors of the building divided by the total buildable site area.

130. Answer: a
IN credit submittal includes proposed requirements, written intent, proposed submittals, and design approach for each proposed innovation credit.

131. Answer: a and b
Light bulbs and batteries are hazardous materials and should be collected at special locations.

Mnemonics for mandatory materials to be collected for recycling:

People Can Make Green Promises

<u>P</u>aper
<u>C</u>ardboard
<u>M</u>etal
<u>G</u>lass
<u>P</u>lastics

See *LEED Green Associate Exam Guide* for more information.

132. Answer: d
 The recycle area should be easily accessible.

133. Answer: c
 Answer "a" is wrong, because if the project team can earn one IN point for this project, they may or may NOT earn one IN point for another project. Having multiple floors is NOT a prerequisite to earn this IN point. The display area does NOT need to include information about every LEED credit awarded to the building, but it does need to be accessible to all occupants of the building in order to qualify for one IN point.

134. Answer: d
 Pay attention the Capital letter in LEED <u>C</u>ertified. This question is included to test your patience.
 Make sure you read ALL the choices of a question before you make a final selection, since some wrong answers look very similar to the correct answer.

135. Answer: b and d
High-albedo pavement can reflect sunlight. Bio-retention ponds can improve microclimate. This means that they are not causes of the heat island effect.

Air-conditioners, vehicle exhaust, dark surfaces, and street equipment are some of the causes of the heat island effect.

136. Answer: d
Pay attention to the correct spelling of potable water, many people mistakenly spell it as portable water. This question also tests your patience.

137. Answer: b and d
These two tasks can be performed by any LEED project team member. Answer "a" is wrong because Mike needs to purchase the USGBC reference guide, which is NOT free, even for other LEED project team members. LEED Online is NOT a database for searching out materials for a LEED project.

138. Answer: b and d
Refer to the MR category credit definition.

139. Answer: a
Answer "d" has some merit, but is not the best answer. The maintenance costs will be higher because of the trees.

140. Answer: b and d
See the free PDF file, "The Treatment by LEED of the Environmental Impact of HVAC Refrigerants," for more information.

141. Answer: c
USGBC and the LEED administrator task force have nothing to do with this issue. The credit will not be denied at the design phase.

142. Answer: d
Increasing the number of floors in a building will reduce the footprint and maximize open spaces.

143. Answer: b and c
Refrigeration and humidifiers use CFCs.

144. Answer: b
Zoning requirements are the most important issue to a project team because they will determine what kind of buildings you can build and may affect many LEED credits. The other choices are important issues, but they are NOT the most important.

145. Answer: a
A LEED scorecard is another name for a LEED credit checklist. A project team needs to refer to the completed LEED scorecard during construction to make sure the project is on track for the intended level of LEED

certification.

146. Answer: c
MPRs serve three goals:
1) To provide clear guidance for customers
2) To maintain LEED program integrity
3) To make the LEED certification process easier

See *LEED Green Associate Exam Guide* for more information.

147. Answer: a, e, and f
See the free PDF file, "The Treatment by LEED of the Environmental Impact of HVAC Refrigerants," for more information.

148. Answer: c
See explanation above.

149. Answer: b, c, and e
Projects outside of the United States can definitely seek and achieve LEED certification. The project team's decision cannot help the project earn points for reducing the heat island effect

150. Answer: a
Proper building orientation is the most important and fundamental factor for energy savings.

151. Answer: b and d
Using adaptive plants is a good practice, but

this choice cannot earn points for alleviation of the heat island effect. Providing shuttle service to bus stations cannot help a project team to earn points for alleviation of the heat island effect either.

152. Answer: d
    The open space credit is no longer tied to presence of a local zoning code. Open spaces must be vegetated and pervious.

153. Answer: b and d
    One can NEVER claim a product is LEED certified because GBCI or USGBC never certify any product. Answer "c" is not as good as Answer "d" because it fails to mention LEED.

154. Answer: c
    Ozone can have negative or positive environmental impacts, depending on where it is located.

155. Answer: d
    All exemplary points are achieved under the Innovation credit.

156. Answer: b
    The energy use for a building (from the most to least): Space heating>Lighting>Cooling>Ventilation

157. Answer: a
A project MUST comply with ALL federal, state, and local codes. They all have precedent over LEED standards.

158. Answer: a
The platted property line of the project is the project boundary. Answer "b" is the property boundary; Answer "c" is the LEED boundary; Answer "d" is a distracter.

159. Answer: e
Greenfields are sites not previously graded or developed that could support habitat, open space, or agriculture.

160. Answer: c and d
The project team can choose to phase out the CFC-based refrigerants before project completion or phase out the CFC-based refrigerants after project completion, as long as the phase out plan is approved by the GBCI.

161. Answer: a
The Clean Air Act requires that no importation or production of HCFCs in the United States will be allowed after 2030.

162. Answer: b

163. Answer: b
LCC focuses on economic analysis while LCA focuses on environmental analysis.

164. Answer: c
Refrigerants with neutral ODP are less efficient.

See the free PDF file, "The Treatment by LEED of the Environmental Impact of HVAC Refrigerants," for more information.

165. Answer: c
Zero extra points will be awarded for a new way, product, or strategy to achieve an existing LEED credit.

166. Answer: c
See the free PDF file, "The Treatment by LEED of the Environmental Impact of HVAC Refrigerants," for more information.

167. Answer: d
The distance to basic services or public transit is determined by walking distance instead of radius, so neither Answer "a" nor Answer "b" is correct. Answers "c" is incorrect because water services and other utilities are on site.

168. Answer: c and e
CFC-based refrigerants can be replaced by natural ventilation or any non-CFC-based refrigerants, including natural refrigerants, HFCs and HCFCs, etc.

169. Answer: c and d
There is a difference between recycling and recycled content. Recycled content is the material containing pre and post consumer content.

170. Answer: d
A LEED AP with a specialty appropriate for the project has to streamline the process of LEED certification, but s/he does NOT have to submit any credits or documents. A Project Administrator is in charge of submitting all credits for final review.

171. Answer: b
At least a one 4-hour Design charrette/workshop shall be conducted no later than the design development stage (preferably at the schematic design stage) to draw on the expertise of all LEED team members.

172. Answer: c and e
The EA category includes a credit for renewable energy production, and the IN category allows an award point for green power if renewable energy accounts for 15% of total energy.

173. Answer: e and f
A building program that details the project's green building requirements includes the green building goals, the project's vision, and a general and room-by-room description

of the project. See *Sustainable Building Technical Manual: Part II*, page 5-6.

Every LEED exam tests project team coordination. Download the free PDF, *Sustainable Building Technical Manual: Part II,* by Anthony Bernheim and William Reed (1996). See the link provided below. Read and memorize it.

http://www.gbci.org/Files/References/Sustainable-Building-Technical-Manual-Part-II.pdf

174. Answer: d
See LT Credit (LTC): Surrounding Density and Diverse Uses

175. Answer: b

176. Answer: a and b
Answer "c" has some merit, but is not as good as Answers "a" and "b."

177. Answer: c
In a phase-out plan, LEED requires reducing the annual leakage rate of the CFC to be 5% or less using EPA Clean Air Act procedures.

Using refrigerants with low ODP and GWP as well as natural refrigerants (including propane) are acceptable for LEED certification.

See the free PDF file, "The Treatment by LEED of the Environmental Impact of HVAC Refrigerants," for more information.

178. Answer: c
All other answers have some merit, but they are not the best answer.

179. Answer: a and c
TARP is Technology Acceptance Reciprocity Partnership. This tool is discussed in the SS category. Green-e is related to the EA category.

The Carpet and Rug Institute's **Green Label Plus** program is in regard to carpet and rugs; The Sheet Metal and Air Conditioning National Contractors Association (SMACNA) has an IAQ Guideline for Occupied Buildings Under Construction; Agrifiber Products is related to EQC: Low-Emitting Materials

180. Answer: b
During construction, a project team should use filtration media with a Minimum Efficiency Reporting Value (MERV) of 8 at each return air grille.

181. Answer: a

182. Answer: c

183. Answer: b

184. Answer: a

Answer "c" is wrong. Savings in landscape irrigation is unlikely because a vegetated roof will probably require more landscape irrigation water than a conventional roof. Answers "b" and "d" are NOT economic benefits.

185. Answer: a

The USGBC logo can be used by organizations approved by USGBC. USGBC members use the USGBC member logo. LEED Green Associates use the LEED Green Associate logo. LEED APs with specialty use a proper LEED AP logo for the related specialty. USGBC Chapters use the USGBC Chapter logo.

186. Answer: c

CIRs can be submitted anytime after the project's registration. A LEED project team should submit CIRs that have already been ruled on with the LEED application to ensure a complete review.

187. Answer: c

CC&R (Covenants, Conditions, and Restrictions), zoning ordinances, and building codes all have more impact on a project's landscape design than the EPAct.

188. Answer: c

Integrated Project Delivery (IPD) is a project delivery approach that integrates <u>business structures, systems, people, and practices</u> into a process that collaboratively harnesses the talents and insights of all participants to <u>reduce waste, increase value to the owner, optimize project results, and maximize efficiency</u> through all phases of design, fabrication, and construction.

See the link below for a <u>free</u> download of "AIA Integrated Project Delivery":

http://www.aia.org/contractdocs/AIAS077630

189. Answer: b

190. Answer: a
See *LEED for Operations and Maintenance Reference Guide-Glossary* (U.S. Green Building Council, 2008):
http://www.gbci.org/Files/References/LEED-for-Operations-and-Maintenance-Reference-Guide-Glossary.pdf

191. Answer: b

192. Answer: a
Pay attention to the word "except."

It should be "unobstructed views located within the distance of *three* times the head height of the vision glazing."

See EQC: Quality Views, or the USGBC reference guide.

193. Answer: a
All other items are related to VOC and IAQ.

194. Answer: a
This is a tricky question. Minimum IAQ Performance is a prerequisite(EQp1), and a point will NOT be awarded.

195. Answer: d
See EQC: Thermal Comfort.

196. Answer: c
Pay attention to the word "except." To minimize building users' exposure to chemical pollutants and possibly dangerous particulates, a project team should provide hard lid ceilings, deck-to-deck partitions, and self-closing doors for copying or printing room, laundry or housekeeping areas, garages, prep rooms, science laboratories, art rooms, (work) shops of any kinds, etc.

Gift shops do NOT have chemical pollutants and possibly dangerous particulates. Therefore, they do not belong to this category of spaces.

197. Answer: b and d

Using composite wood and agrifiber products can affect LEED credit categories, EQ and MR.

198. Answer: a and b

SCAQMD and Green Seal are related to the EQ category.

For EQC: Low-Emitting Materials, all adhesives and sealants wet-applied on site must meet the applicable chemical content requirements of SCAQMD Rule 1168, July 1, 2005, Adhesive and Sealant Applications, as analyzed by the methods specified in Rule 1168.

Green Seal certification is used to identify lead- and cadmium-free paints for metal-free paints or an equivalent source of lead- and cadmium-free documentation.

Green-e certified products are related to EA category.

The Carpet and Rug Institute's Green Label Plus program is in regard to carpet and rugs.

199. Answer: a and c
BUG means the backlight-uplight-glare. MLO stands for Model Lighting Ordinance. LUG and MLH are distracters, and do not exist.

200. Answer: b
Pay attention to the word "except." Building orientation can contribute to optimizing energy performance, better natural ventilation, and passive solar heating. It will not contribute to EAC: Green Power and Carbon Offsets (off-site renewable energy). On-site renewable energy is covered under another credit, EAC: Renewable Energy Production.

IV. How were the LEED Green Associate Mock Exams created?

The actual LEED Green Associate Exam has 100 questions and you must finish it within two hours. The raw exam score is converted to a scaled score ranging from 125 to 200. The passing score is 170 or higher.

I tried to be scientific when selecting the mock exam questions, so I based the number of questions for each credit category roughly on the number of points that you can get for that category, otherwise known as LEED Credit Weighting. See detailed discussion below. The difficulty level for each question was designed to match the real exam and the sample questions that can be downloaded from the official GBCI website.

If you answered 60 of the 100 questions correctly, you have passed the mock exam.

Many readers who took the exam commented on the fact that there are MANY questions on refrigerants.

This has a lot to do with LEED v4 Credit Weighting. EA (including refrigerants) is the biggest winner in LEED v4, meaning the category has MORE questions than any other areas for ALL the LEED exams. See portion of my book, *LEED Green Associate Exam Guide* quoted below:

How are LEED credits allocated and weighted?
Answer: Credits that can contribute to LEED's **"Impact Categories"** are given more points. These impact categories are weighted through a consensus driven process:
- Global **Climate Change** (35%)
- Social Equity, Environmental Justice, and **Community** Quality of Life (5%)
- Individual **Human Health** and well-being (20%)
- **Greener Economy** (5%)
- **Biodiversity** and Ecosystem (10%)
- **Water Resources** (15%)
- Sustainable and Regenerative **Material Resources** Cycles (10%)

The USGBC uses three **association factors** to measure and scale credit outcome to a given Impact Category component:
- **Relative Efficacy:** It measures whether a credit outcome has a positive or negative association with a given Impact Category component, and how strong that association is.
  - No association
  - Low association
  - Medium association
  - High association
  - Negative association

- **Benefit Duration:** How long will the benefits or consequences of the credit outcome last?

- 1-3 Years
- 4-10 Years
- 11-30 Years
- 30+ Years (Building/Community Lifetime)

• **Controllability of Effect:** It indicates which individual is most directly responsible for achieving the expected credit outcome. The more a credit outcome depends on active human effort, the less likely it will be achieved with certainty, and the credit will have fewer pints, vice versa.

The USGBC simplifies the weighting process of points into a score **card**:
- **100 base points** for the base LEED Rating System
- **1 point minimum** for each credit
- **Whole points** and no fractions for LEED points.

See detailed discussions at the FREE PDF file entitled "LEED v4 Impact Category and Point Allocation Development Process" at the following link:
http://www.usgbc.org/sites/default/files/LEED%20v4%20Impact%20Category%20and%20Point%20Allocation%20Process_Overview_0.pdf

V. Where can I find the latest official sample questions for the LEED Green Associate Exam?

Answer: You can find them, as well as the exam content, from the candidate handbook, at: http://www.usgbc.org/resources/list/credentialing-resources

VI. LEED Green Associate Exam registration

1. How do I register for the LEED Green Associate Exam?

Answer: Per the GBCI, you must create an Eligibility ID at www.GBCI.org. Select the "Schedule an Exam" menu to set up an exam time and date with Prometric. You can reschedule or cancel the LEED Green Associate Exam at www.prometric.com/gbci with your Prometric-issued confirmation number for the exam. You need to bring two forms of ID to the exam site. See www.prometric/gbci for a list of exam sites. Call 1-800-795-1747 (within the United States) or 202-742-3792 (Outside of the United States) or e-mail exam@gbci.org if you have any questions.

2. **Important Note:** You can download the "LEED Green Associate Candidate Handbook" from the GBCI website for information on all the <u>latest</u> details and procedures. Ideally you should download and carefully read this handbook at least <u>three</u> weeks before your exam. See the link below:
http://www.usgbc.org/resources/list/credentialing-resources

Chapter 3
Frequently Asked Questions (FAQ) and Other Useful Resources

The following are tips on how to pass the LEED exam on the first try and in one week. I also included my responses to some readers' questions. They may help you:

1. **I found the reference guide way too tedious. Can I read your books only and just refer to the USGBC reference guide (if one is available for the exam I am taking) when needed?**

    Response: Yes, that is one way to study. If you read only *LEED Green Associate Exam Guide*, you already have a very good chance of passing. *LEED GREEN ASSOCIATE Mock Exams* will help you become more familiar with the way that questions are asked in the real LEED Green Associate Exam, give you more confidence, and increase your chance of passing.

2. **Is one week really enough time for me to prepare for the exam while I am working?**

    Response: Yes, if you can put in 40 to 60 hours study time during the week you can pass the exam. This exam is similar to a history or political science exam; you need to MEMORIZE the information. If you wait too long to take the test after studying, you will probably forget the information.

In my book, *LEED Green Associate Exam Guide*, I give you tips on how to MEMORIZE the information, and I have already highlighted/underlined the most important materials that you definitely have to MEMORIZE in order to pass the exam. My goal through this book is to help you to pass the LEED Green Associate Exam with minimum time and effort. I want to make your life easier.

However, to be on the safe side, for an average reader, I recommend not less than 2 weeks, but not MORE than 2 months of prep time.

3. Would you say that if I buy books from your LEED Exam Guide series, I could pass the exam without any other study materials? The books sold on the USGBC website cost hundreds of dollars, so I would be quite happy if I could buy your books and just use them.

Response: First of all, there are readers who have passed the LEED exam by reading only my books in the LEED Exam Guide series (www.GreenExamEducation.com). My goal is to write one book for each of the LEED exams, and make each of my books stand alone to prepare people for one specific LEED exam.

Secondly, people learn in many different ways. That is why I published *LEED GREEN ASSOCIATE Mock Exams*, and added some new advice below for people who learn better by doing practice tests.

If you do the following things, you have a very good chance of passing the LEED exam (This is NOT a guarantee, nobody can guarantee you will pass):

a. If you study, understand, and MEMORIZE all of the information in my book, *LEED Green Associate Exam Guide*, do NOT panic when you run into problems you are unfamiliar with, and use the guess strategy explained in my books, then you have a very good chance of passing the exam.

You need to UNDERSTAND and MEMORIZE the information in *LEED Green Associate Exam Guide* and achieve almost a perfect score on the mock exam in order to pass the GA exam or the first part of any AP exam. For the second part of the specific LEED AP exam you are taking, the corresponding book from my LEED Exam Guide series will give you the BULK of the most CURRENT information that you need. You *have to* know the information included in my book related to the specific AP Exam you are taking, in order to pass the second part of the AP Exam.

b. If you have not been involved in any LEED projects before, I suggest you also go to the USGBC website, and download the latest LEED credit templates for the LEED rating system related to the LEED exam you are taking. Read the templates and become familiar with them. This is important. See the link below:
http://www.usgbc.org/leed#rating

c. If you want to be safe and take additional sample tests to find out if you are ready for the real Green Associate Exam or part one of the AP exam, I would suggest *LEED GREEN ASSOCIATE Mock Exams*. That is probably the reason you bought this book in the first place.

In fact, some of my readers have passed the LEED Green Associate Exam with a high score by reading only my books, *LEED Green Associate Exam Guide* and *LEED GREEN ASSOCIATE Mock Exams* and WITHOUT reading the USGBC reference guide AT ALL.

The LEED exam is NOT an easy exam, but anyone with a 7th grade education should be able to study and pass the LEED exam if s/he prepares correctly.

If you have extra time and money, the only other book I would recommend is the USGBC reference guide. I know some people who did not even read the reference guide from cover to cover when they took the exam. They just studied the information in my book, only referred to the reference guide to look up a few things, and passed on the first try. Some of my readers have even passed WITHOUT reading the USGBC reference guide AT ALL.

4. I am preparing for the LEED exam. Do I need to read the 2" thick reference guide?

Response: See the answer above.

5. For LEED v4, will the total number of points be more than 110 if a project receives all of the extra and standard credits?

Response: No, for LEED v4, there are <u>100</u> base points and <u>10</u> possible bonus points. There are many ways to achieve bonus points (extra credits or exemplary performance), but you can have a maximum number of only <u>6 IN</u> and <u>4 Regional Priority</u> bonus points. So, the maximum points for ANY project will be <u>110</u>.

6. For the exam, do I need to know the project phase in which a specific prerequisite/credit takes place? i.e., pre-design, schematic design, etc.

Response: The information on the project phase (NOT LEED submittal phase) for each prerequisite/credit is NOT mentioned in the USGBC reference guides, but it is covered in the USGBC workshops. If this information is important enough for the USGBC workshops to cover, then it may show up on the actual LEED exam.

Most, if not all, other third-party books completely miss this important information. I cover the material for each prerequisite/credit in my book because I think it is very important.

Some people THINK that the LEED exam ONLY tests information covered by the USGBC reference guides. They are wrong.

The LEED exam does test information NOT covered by the USGBC reference guides at all. This may include the process of LEED submittal and project team coordination, etc.

I would MEMORIZE this information if I were you, because it may show up on the LEED exam. Besides, this information is not hard to memorize once you understand the content, and you need to know it to do actual LEED submittal work anyway.

7. **Are you writing any other books for the new LEED exams? What new books are you writing?**

    Response: Yes, I am working on other books in the LEED Exam Guide series. I will be writing one book for each of the LEED exams. See GreenExamEducation.com for more information.

8. Important Documents that You Need to Download for <u>Free</u>, Become Familiar with, and <u>Memorize</u>

Note: GBCI and USGBC change the links to their documents every now and then, so, by the time you read this book, they may have changed some of the following links. You can simply go to their main website, search for the document by name, and should be able to find the most current link. You can use the same technique to search for documents by other organizations.

The main website for GBCI is:
http://www.gbci.org/

The main website for USGBC is:
http://www.usgbc.org/

a. **Every** LEED exam **tests** Credit Interpretation Request/Rulings (CIR). Download the related document, read, and <u>memorize</u>:
http://www.gbci.org/Certification/Resources/cirs.aspx

b. **Every** LEED exam **tests** project team coordination. Download *Sustainable Building Technical Manual: Part II,* by Anthony Bernheim and William Reed (1996), read and <u>memorize</u>:
http://www.gbci.org/Files/References/Sustainable-Building-Technical-Manual-Part-II.pdf

c. Project Registration Application and LEED Certification Process: http://www.usgbc.org/certification

d. LEED Online: https://leedonline.usgbc.org/Login.aspx

9. Important Documents that You Need to Download for <u>Free</u>, and Become <u>Familiar</u> with

a. *LEED for Operations and Maintenance Reference Guide-Introduction* (U.S. Green Building Council, 2013): http://www.usgbc.org/sites/all/assets/section/files/v4-guide-excerpts/Excerpt_v4_OM.pdf

b. *LEED for Operations and Maintenance Reference Guide-Glossary* (U.S. Green Building Council, 2008): http://www.gbci.org/Files/References/LEED-for-Operations-and-Maintenance-Reference-Guide-Glossary.pdf

c. *LEED for Homes Rating System* (U.S. Green Building Council, 2008): http://www.gbci.org/Files/References/LEED-for-Homes-Rating-System.pdf

    Pay special attention to the list of **abbreviations and acronyms** on pages 105–106 and the helpful **glossary of terms** on pages 107–114.

d. *Cost of Green Revisited,* by Davis Langdon

(2007): http://www.gbci.org/Files/References/Cost-of-Green-Revisited.pdf

e. *The Treatment by LEED® of the Environmental Impact of HVAC Refrigerants* (LEED Technical and Scientific Advisory Committee, 2004): http://www.gbci.org/Files/References/The-Treatment-by-LEED-of-the-Environmental-Impact-of-HVAC-Refrigerants.pdf

f. *Guidance on Innovation and Design (ID) Credits* (US Green Building Council, 2004): http://www.gbci.org/Files/References/Guidance-on-Innovation-and-Design-Credits.pdf

Appendixes

1. **Default occupancy factors**

Occupancy	Gross sf per occupant	
	Transient Occupant	**FTE**
Educational, Daycare	630	105
Educational, K–12	1,300	140
Educational, Postsecondary	2,100	150
Grocery store	550	115
Hotel	1,500	700
Laboratory or R&D	400	0
Office, Medical	225	330
Office, General	250	0
Retail, General	550	130
Retail or Service (auto, financial, etc.)	600	130
Restaurant	435	95
Warehouse, Distribution	2,500	0
Warehouse, Storage	20,000	0

Note: This table is for projects (like CS) where the final occupant count is not available. If your project's occupancy factors are not listed above, you can use a comparable building to show the average gross sf per occupant for your building's use.

2. Important Resources and Further Study Materials You Can Download for <u>Free</u> or at a Low Price

Note: GBCI and USGBC change the links to their documents every now and then, so, by the time you read this book, they may have changed some of the following links. You can simply go to their main website, search for the document by name, and you should be able to find the most current link. You can use the same technique to search for documents by other organizations.

The main website for GBCI is:
http://www.gbci.org/

The main website for USGBC is:
http://www.usgbc.org/

Energy Performance of LEED® for New Construction Buildings: Final Report, by Cathy Turner and Mark Frankel (2008):
http://www.gbci.org/Files/References/Energy-Performance-of-LEED-for-New-Construction-Buildings-Final-Report.pdf

Foundations of the Leadership in Energy and Environmental Design Environmental Rating System: A Tool for Market Transformation (LEED Steering Committee, 2006):
http://www.gbci.org/Files/References/Foundations-of-the-Leadership-in-Energy-and-Environmental-Design-Environmental-Rating-System-A-Tool-for-Market-Transformation.pdf

AIA Integrated Project Delivery: A Guide (www.aia.org):
http://www.aia.org/contractdocs/AIAS077630

Review of ANSI/ASHRAE Standard 62.1-2004: Ventilation for Acceptable Indoor Air Quality, by Brian Kareis:
http://www.workplace-hygiene.com/articles/ANSI-ASHRAE-3.html

Best Practices of ISO - 14021: Self-Declared Environmental Claims, by Kun-Mo Lee and Haruo Uehara (2003):
http://books.google.be/books/about/Best_practices_of_ISO_14021.html?hl=nl&id=e2eCAAAACAAJ

Bureau of Labor Statistics (www.bls.gov)

International Code Council (www.iccsafe.org)

Americans with Disabilities Act (ADA): Standards for Accessible Design (www.ada.gov):
http://www.ada.gov/stdspdf.htm

GSA Facilities Standards (General Services Administration, Latest Edition):
http://www.gsa.gov/portal/content/104821

Guide to Purchasing Green Power (Environmental Protection Agency, 2004):
http://www.gbci.org/Files/References/Guide-to-Purchasing-Green-Power.pdf

USGBC Definitions:
https://www.usgbc.org/ShowFile.aspx?DocumentID=5744

3. Annotated Bibliography

Chen, Gang. ***LEED Green Associate Exam Guide***: *A Must-Have for the LEED Green Associate Exam: Comprehensive Study Materials, Sample Questions, Mock Exam, Green Building LEED Certification, and Sustainability (Latest Edition)*. This is a very comprehensive and concise book on the LEED Green Associate Exam. Some readers have passed the LEED Green Associate Exam by studying this book for three days.

4. Valuable Websites and Links

a. The Official Websites for the U.S. Green Building Council (USGBC):
http://www.usgbc.org/
http://www.Greenbuild365.org

Pay special attention to the purpose of LEED Online, LEED project registration, LEED certification content, LEED reference guide introductions, LEED rating systems, and checklists.

You can download or purchase the following useful documents from the USGBC or GBCI website:

Latest and official LEED exam candidate handbooks including an exam content outline and sample questions:
http://www.usgbc.org/resources/list/credentialing-resources

LEED Reference Guides:
http://www.usgbc.org/leed/v4

LEED Rating System Selection:
http://www.usgbc.org/certification

Read the document above <u>at least three times</u>, because it is VERY important, and tells you which LEED system to use.

Various versions of LEED Green Building Rating Systems and Project Checklist:
http://www.usgbc.org/leed/v4

b. Natural Resources Defense Council:
http://www.nrdc.org/

c. Environmental Construction + Design - Green Book (Offers print magazine and on-line environmental products and services resources guide):
http://www.edcmag.com/greenbook

d. Cool Roof Rating Council website:
http://www.coolroofs.org

Back Page Promotion

You may be interested in some other books written by Gang Chen:

1. ***Architectural Practice Simplified:** A Survival Guide and Checklists for Building Construction and Site Improvements as well as Tips on Architecture, Building Design, Construction and Project Management* (Published on December 23, 2009): http://www.GreenExamEducation.com

2. ***Planting Design Illustrated:** A Must-Have for Landscape Architecture: A Holistic Garden Design Guide with Architectural and Horticultural Insight, and Ideas from Famous Gardens in Major Civilizations* (Latest Edition): http://www.GreenExamEducation.com

3. **LEED Exam Guide series.** Refer to the link below: http://www.GreenExamEducation.com

Note: Other books in the LEED Exam Guide series are currently in production. One book will eventually be produced for each of the LEED exams. The series includes:
***LEED GREEN ASSOCIATE EXAM GUIDE:** A Must-Have for the LEED Green Associate Exam: Comprehensive Study Materials, Sample Questions, Mock Exam, Green Building LEED Certification, and Sustainability (Latest Edition)*, Book 2, LEED Exam Guide series, GreenExamEducation.com

LEED BD&C EXAM GUIDE: A Must-Have for the LEED AP BD+C Exam: Comprehensive Study Materials, Sample Questions, Mock Exam, Green Building Design and Construction, LEED Certification, and Sustainability (Latest Edition), Book 3, LEED Exam Guide series, GreenExamEducation.com

LEED ID&C EXAM GUIDE: A Must-Have for the LEED AP ID+C Exam: Comprehensive Study Materials, Sample Questions, Mock Exam, Green Interior Design and Construction, LEED Certification, and Sustainability (Latest Edition), Book 4, LEED Exam Guide series, GreenExamEducation.com

LEED O&M EXAM GUIDE: A Must-Have for the LEED AP O+M Exam: Comprehensive Study Materials, Sample Questions, Mock Exam, Green Building Operations and Maintenance, LEED Certification, and Sustainability (Latest Edition), Book 5, LEED Exam Guide series, GreenExamEducation.com

LEED HOMES EXAM GUIDE: A Must-Have for the LEED AP+ Homes Exam: Comprehensive Study Materials, Sample Questions, Mock Exam, Green Building LEED Certification, and Sustainability (Latest Edition), Book 6, LEED Exam Guide series, GreenExamEducation.com

LEED ND EXAM GUIDE: A Must-Have for the LEED AP+ Neighborhood Development Exam: Comprehensive Study Materials, Sample Questions, Mock Exam, Green Building LEED Certification, and Sustainability (Latest Edition), Book 7, LEED Exam Guide series, GreenExamEducation.com

LEED GREEN ASSOCIATE MOCK EXAMS: Questions, Answers and Explanation: A Must-Have for the LEED Green Associate Exam, Green Building LEED Certification, and Sustainability (Latest Edition), Book 8, LEED Exam Guide series, GreenExamEducation.com

LEED AP EXAM GUIDE: Study Materials, Sample Questions, Mock Exam, Building LEED Certification (LEED-NC) and Going Green, Book 1, LEED Exam Guide series, GreenExamEducation.com

How to order these books:
You can order the books listed above at:
http://www.GreenExamEducation.com

OR
http://amazon.com

OR
Any other Amazon site, such as http://amazon.ca, http://amazon.co.uk, http://amazon.co.jp, etc.

OR
http://bn.com

Following are some detailed descriptions of each text:

LEED Exam Guide series

Comprehensive Study Materials, Sample Questions, Mock Exam, Building LEED Certification, and Going Green

LEED (Leadership in Energy and Environmental Design) is the most important trend in development and is revolutionizing the construction industry. It has gained tremendous momentum and has a profound impact on our environment. From the LEED Exam Guide series, you will learn how to:

1. Pass the LEED Green Associate Exam and various other LEED AP+ exams (each book will help you with a specific LEED exam).

2. Register and certify a building for LEED certification.

3. Understand the intent of each LEED prerequisite and credit.

4. Calculate points for a LEED credit.

5. Identify the responsible party for each prerequisite and credit.

6. Earn extra credits (exemplary performance) for LEED.

7. Implement the local codes and building standards for prerequisites and credits.

8. Receive points for categories not yet clearly defined by the USGBC.

There is currently NO official GBCI book on the LEED Green Associate Exam, and most of the existing books on LEED and LEED AP+ are too expensive and too complicated to be practical or helpful. The pocket guides in the LEED Exam Guide series fill in the blanks, demystify LEED, and uncover the tips, codes, and jargon for LEED as well as the true meaning of "going green." They will set up a solid foundation and fundamental framework of LEED for you. Each book in the LEED Exam Guide series covers every aspect of one or more specific LEED rating systems in plain and concise language, and makes this information understandable to anyone.

These pocket guides are small and easy to carry. You can read them whenever you have a few extra minutes. They are indispensable books for everyone: administrators; developers; contractors; architects; landscape architects; civil, mechanical, electrical, and plumbing engineers; interns; drafters; designers; and other design professionals.

Why is the LEED Exam Guide series Needed?

A number of books are available that you can use to prepare for the LEED exams:

1. USGBC reference guides. You need to select the correct version of the reference guide for your exam.

The USGBC reference guides are comprehensive, but they give too much information. For example, *The LEED Reference Guide for Green Building Design and Construction v4 (BD&C)* has 817 oversized pages. Many of the calculations in the books are too detailed for the exam. They are also expensive (approximately $250 each, so most people may not buy them for their personal use, but instead, will seek to share an office copy).

Reading a reference guide from cover to cover is good if you have the time. The problem is that very few people actually have the time to read the whole reference guide. Even if you do read the whole guide, you may not remember the important issues required to pass the LEED exam. You need to reread the material several times before you can remember much of it.

Reading a reference guide from cover to cover without a guidebook is a difficult and inefficient way of preparing for the LEED exams, because you do NOT know what USGBC and GBCI are looking for in the exam.

2. The USGBC workshops and related handouts are concise, but they do not cover extra credits (exemplary performance). The workshops are expensive, costing approximately $500 each.

3. Various books published by third parties are available on Amazon. However, most of them are not very helpful.

There are many books on LEED, but few are useful.

Each book in the LEED Exam Guide series will fill in the blanks and become a valuable, reliable source:

a. They will give you more information for your money. Each of the books in the LEED Exam Guide series has more information than the related USGBC workshops.

b. They are exam-oriented and more effective than the USGBC reference guides.

c. They are better than most, if not all, of the other third-party books. They give you comprehensive study materials, sample questions and answers, mock exams and answers, and critical information on building LEED certification and going green. Other third-party books only give you a fraction of the information.

d. They are comprehensive yet concise. They are small and easy to carry around. You can read them whenever you have a few extra minutes.

e. They are great timesavers. I have highlighted the important information that you need to understand and MEMORIZE. I also make some acronyms and short sentences to help you easily remember the credit names.

You should devote about 1 to 2 weeks of full-time study to pass each of the LEED exams. I have met people who have spent only 40 hours of study time, and passed the exams.

You can find sample texts and other information about the LEED Exam Guide series listed under the Amazon customer discussion section for each available book.

What Others Are Saying About *LEED Green Associate Exam Guide* (Book 2, LEED Exam Guide series).

"Finally! A comprehensive study tool for LEED GREEN ASSOCIATE Prep!
"I took the 1-day Green LEED Green Associate course and walked away with a power point binder printed in very small print—which was missing MUCH of the required information (although I didn't know it at the time). I studied my little heart out and took the test, only to fail it by 1 point. Turns out I did NOT study all the material I needed to in order to pass the test. I found this book, read it, marked it up, retook the test, and passed it with a 95%. Look, we all know the LEED Green Associate exam is new and the resources for study are VERY limited. This one's the VERY best out there right now. I highly recommend it."
—ConsultantVA

"Complete overview for the LEED Green Associate exam
"I studied this book for about 3 days and passed the exam ... if you are truly interested in learning about the LEED system and green building design, this is a great place to start."
—K.A. Evans

"Very effective study guide
"I purchased both this study guide and Mr. Chen's LEED GREEN ASSOCIATE Mock Exams book and found them to be excellent tools for preparing for the LEED Green Associate exam. While Mr. Chen's LEED Green Associate Exam Guide is not perfect (in that it's not the most user-friendly presentation of the material), it was very effective in at least presenting most, if not all, of the topics that the exam touched upon. While I wouldn't necessarily recommend my abbreviated strategy for preparing for the exam, the following worked for me: I read through the exam guide a couple of times (but not word for word), took the mock exam and referenced the guide for explanations for any wrong answers, did the same for the two mock exams in Mr. Chen's LEED GREEN ASSOCIATE Mock Exams book, flipped through the documents that Mr. Chen recommends, and took two other web-based mock exams that I purchased on eBay. Literally after ten hours of preparation time, I took the actual exam and passed with a 189, thanks in large part to Mr. Chen's books. If I decide to take one of the LEED AP exams in the future, I will definitely be picking up more of Mr. Chen's study materials."
—shwee "shwee"

"Only study guide needed to pass on your first try
"I don't write reviews, but I'm compelled to for this purchase. This was the only book I read and studied to prepare for the LEED Green Associate exam, and passed with ease on the first try today. I was over prepared for the exam by using this study guide,

which is what I wanted on exam day. I bought the book, read it 3 times, learned a lot of good information, saved valuable time, and passed on the first try. By the way, I'm not a good test taker. I don't agree with any of the negative reviews that are posted... I'm glad I ignored those when I made the purchase and went with the majority. THIS PRODUCT DELIVERED THE RESULTS, CASE CLOSED. I'll be buying his *LEED AP BD&C Exam Guide* to prepare for the specialty exam. Thank you Mr. Gang Chen !!!"
—Lobo

"I just finished taking the LEED Green Associate exam and, thankfully, I passed it on the first try by using this book as my primary study guide...I particularly liked the way the author organized the information within it."
—Lewis Colon

Architectural Practice Simplified

A Survival Guide and Checklists for Building Construction and Site Improvements as well as Tips on Architecture, Building Design, Construction, and Project Management

Learn the Tips, Become One of Those Who Know Architectural Practice, and Thrive in the Construction Industry!

For architectural practice, building design, and the construction industry, there are two kinds of people: those who know, and those who don't. The tips about building design, construction, and project management have been kept to those who know, until now.

Most of the existing books on architectural practice are too expensive, too complicated, and too long to be practical or helpful. This book simplifies the process to make it easier to understand and uncovers the tips of building design as well as construction and project management. It sets up a solid foundation and fundamental framework for this field. It covers every aspect of architectural practice in plain and concise language that makes the information accessible to all people. Through practical case studies, the text demonstrates the efficient and proper ways to handle various issues and problems that arise in architectural practice, building design, and the construction industry.

The book is for ordinary people, aspiring young architects, as well as seasoned professionals in the construction industry. For ordinary people, it uncovers the tips of building construction; for aspiring architects, it works as a construction industry survival guide and a guidebook to shorten the process of mastering architectural practice and climbing up the professional ladder. For seasoned architects, it has many checklists for refreshing memory. It is an indispensable reference book for ordinary people, architectural students, interns, drafters, designers, seasoned architects, construction administrators, superintendents, construction managers, contractors, and developers.

You will learn:
1. How to develop your business and work with your client.
2. The entire process of building design and construction, including programming, entitlement, schematic design, design development, construction documents, bidding, and construction administration.
3. How to coordinate with government agencies, such as a county's health department or a city's planning, building, fire, or public works department.
4. How to coordinate with your consultants, including soils, civil, structural, electrical, mechanical, plumbing engineers, landscape architects, etc.

5. How to create and use your own checklists to provide quality control of your construction documents.
6. How to use various logs (i.e., RFI log, submittal log, field visit log, etc.) and lists (contact list, document control list, distribution list, etc.) to organize and simplify your work.
7. How to respond to RFI issues, CCDs, and review change orders, submittals, etc.
8. How to make your architectural practice a profitable and successful business.

Planting Design Illustrated
A Must-Have for Landscape Architecture
A Holistic Garden Design Guide with
Architectural and Horticultural Insight,
and Ideas from Famous Gardens
in Major Civilizations

One of the most significant books on landscaping!

This is one of the most comprehensive books on planting design. It fills in the blanks of the field and introduces poetry, painting, and symbolism into planting design. It covers in detail the two major systems of planting design: formal planting design and naturalistic planting design. It has numerous line drawings and photos to illustrate the planting design concepts and principles. Through in-depth discussions of historical precedents and practical case studies, it uncovers the fundamental design principles and concepts, as well as the underpinning philosophy for planting design. It is an indispensable reference book for landscape architecture students, designers, architects, urban planners, and ordinary garden lovers.

What Others Are Saying About *Planting Design Illustrated* ...

"I found this book to be absolutely fascinating. You will need to concentrate while reading it, but the effort will be well worth your time."
—Bobbie Schwartz, former president of APLD (Association of Professional Landscape Designers) and author of *The Design Puzzle: Putting the Pieces Together*.

"This is a book that you have to read, and it is more than well worth your time. Gang Chen takes you well beyond what you will learn in other books about basic principles like color, texture, and mass."
—Jane Berger, editor & publisher of gardendesignonline

"As a long-time consumer of gardening books, I am impressed with Gang Chen's inclusion of new information on planting design theory for Chinese and Japanese gardens. Many gardening books discuss the beauty of Japanese gardens, and a few discuss the unique charms of Chinese gardens, but this one explains how Japanese and Chinese history, as well as geography and artistic traditions, bear on the development of each country's style. The material on traditional Western garden planting is thorough and inspiring, too. *Planting Design Illustrated* definitely rewards repeated reading and study. Any garden designer will read it with profit."
—Jan Whitner, editor of the *Washington Park Arboretum Bulletin*

"Enhanced with an annotated bibliography and informative appendices, *Planting Design Illustrated* offers an especially "reader friendly" and practical guide that makes it a very strongly recommended addition to personal, professional, academic, and community library gardening & landscaping reference collection and supplemental reading list."
—Midwest Book Review

"Where to start? *Planting Design Illustrated* is, above all, fascinating and refreshing! Not something the lay reader encounters everyday, the book presents an unlikely topic in an easily digestible, easy-to-follow way. It is superbly organized with a comprehensive table of contents, bibliography, and appendices. The writing, though expertly informative, maintains its accessibility throughout and is a joy to read. The detailed and beautiful illustrations expanding on the concepts presented were my favorite portion. One of the finest books I've encountered in this contest in the past 5 years."
—Writer's Digest 16th Annual International Self-Published Book Awards Judge's Commentary

"The work in my view has incredible application to planting design generally and a system approach to what is a very difficult subject to teach, at least in my experience. Also featured is a very beautiful philosophy of garden design principles bordering poetry. It's my strong conviction that this work needs to see the light of day by being published for the use of professionals, students & garden enthusiasts."

—Donald C Brinkerhoff, FASLA, chairman and CEO of Lifescapes International, Inc.

Index

40/60 rule for LEED, 63
Albedo, 30, 45, 72
American Council for an Energy Efficient Economy (ACEEE), 61, 63
ammonia (NH3), 50
Basic Services, 70
blackwater, 28, 52, 57, 74, 77, 93
BUG, 113, 134
CFC, 27, 33, 34, 45, 49, 50, 56, 61, 62, 72, 73, 75, 76, 82, 86, 87, 91, 95, 96, 100, 101, 103, 106, 116, 117, 123, 126, 127, 129
CIRs, 42, 51, 69, 77, 93, 104, 108, 109, 131
Cradle-to-cradle, 44, 71
Energy Policy Act (EPAct), 29, 58
FAR, 27, 40, 56, 67, 91, 106, 120
FTE, 151
graywater, 28, 34, 44, 52, 57, 62, 71, 78, 88, 93
Green-e, 30, 33, 45, 59, 61, 85, 107, 112, 116, 130
GWP, 42, 49, 50, 69, 74, 75, 76, 83, 94, 102, 106, 114, 129
Halon, 34, 62
LEED Rating System Selection Policy, 64, 155
Life cycle analysis, 44, 83, 114
Life cycle cost analysis, 83, 114
MERV, 130
MLO, 113, 134
Mnemonics, 65, 120
MPRs, 124
ODP, 35, 42, 47, 49, 50, 69, 74, 75, 76, 83, 86, 87, 94, 96, 99, 102, 106, 114, 116, 127, 129

Open spaces, 60, 114, 125
process energy, 26, 53, 55, 78
RECs, 45, 72, 84, 115
Regional Priority, 30, 58, 84, 89, 116, 145
regulated (non-process) energy, 26, 55, 79

ROI, 38, 65
SRI, 30, 36, 43, 45, 59, 69, 72
stormwater, 27, 36, 43, 56, 63, 69, 94
Zero Emission Vehicles (ZEV), 34, 61

www.ingramcontent.com/pod-product-compliance
Lightning Source LLC
Chambersburg PA
CBHW060955230426
43665CB00015B/2208